Introduction ii
Syllabus Coverage Overview iii

1	Place Value 1	1
2	Number Crunching 1	12
3	Number Crunching 2	23
4	Estimating	33
5	Patterns	40
6	Shapes 1	46
7	Shapes 2	50
8	Directions	56
9	Units 1	64
10	Graphs and Tables 1	71
11	Place Value 2	81
12	Rounding	87
13	Number Crunching 3	93
14	Number Crunching 4	101
15	Decimals 1	107
16	Money	114
17	Negative Numbers	123
18	Number Machines	129
19	Symmetry 1	136
20	Symmetry 2	143
21	Angles	151
22	Units 2	157
23	Decimals 2	165
24	Time 1	175
25	Graphs and Tables 2	184
26	Chance	191
27	Multiply 10, Divide 10	196
28	Fractions ,	203
29	Percentages	212
30	Finding Rules	219
31	Backwards Calculations	229
32	Formulas	234
33	Co-ordinates	242
34	Filling Space	248
35	Time 2	259
36	Averages	267

Introduction

	Chapter	Summary of Chapter Content	N.C. Level Attained	Page
1	Place Value 1	numbers to a thousand	A.T. 2.2/3	1
2	Number Crunching 1	addition and subtraction of two-digit numbers	A.T. 2.2/3	12
3	Number Crunching 2	multiplication and division by 2, 5 and 10	A.T. 2.2/3	23
4	Estimating	estimating length, weight, size and time	A.T. 2.3	33
5	Patterns	pattern in number and shape	A.T. 2.2/3	40
6	Shapes 1	names and characteristics of 2-D and 3-D shapes	A.T. 3.2	46
7	Shapes 2	properties of 3-D shapes	A.T. 3.2	50
8	Directions	words and appropriate metric units	A.T. 3.2	56
9	Units 1	using words and units to measure	A.T. 3.2	64
10	Graphs and Tables 1	tables, charts and diagrams to show information	A.T. 4.2/3	71
11	Place Value 2	numbers to one million	A.T. 2.4	81
12	Rounding	to the nearest ten and hundred	A.T. 2.3	87
13	Number Crunching 3	four-number rules to one thousand	A.T. 2.4	93
14	Number Crunching 4	using a calculator to solve problems	A.T. 2.4	101
15	Decimals 1	decimals and decimal scales to one place	A.T. 2.4	107
16	Money	money and sums to £10	A.T. 2.4	114
17	Negative Numbers	negative numbers and sums from 10 to −10	A.T. 2.3/4	123
18	Number Machines	using one- and two-number machines	A.T. 2.3	129
19	Symmetry 1	reflection in 2-D	A.T. 3.4	136
20	Symmetry 2	rotation, translation and congruence in 2-D	A.T. 3.2/4	143
21	Angles	labelling angle types and measuring	A.T. 3.5	151
22	Units 2	converting units	A.T. 3.3	157
23	Decimals 2	decimals and decimal scales to two places	A.T. 3.4	165
24	Time 1	clockfaces and units of time	A.T. 3.4	175
25	Graphs and Tables 2	extracting from tables and drawing graphs	A.T. 4.3/4	184
26	Chance	words we use to describe the chance of something happing	A.T. 4.4	191
27	Multiply 10, Divide 10	multiplying and dividing by 10 and 100	A.T. 4.4	196
28	Fractions	shading fractions and fraction of a quantity	A.T. 2.4	203
29	Percentages	simple percentages and percentage of a quantity	A.T. 2.4	212
30	Finding Rules	finding patterns and their connecting rules	A.T. 2.4	219
31	Backwards Calculations	reversing single and double sums	A.T. 2.4	229
32	Formulas	formulas in words and numbers	A.T. 2.4	234
33	Co-ordinates	co-ordinates in the first quadrant	A.T. 2.4	242
34	Filling Space	perimeter, area and volume by counting	A.T. 3.4	248
35	Time 2	12–24 hour clocks and timetables	A.T. 3.4	259
36	Averages	average, mode, median and range	A.T. 4.4	267

Syllabus Coverage Overview

Chapter		WJEC	NEAB	CCEA	SEG	MEG	Page
1	Place Value 1	Mod 1	Unit 1+2	Bronze	Core	Core	1
2	Number Crunching 1	Mod 1	Unit 1+2	Bronze	Core	Core	12
3	Number Crunching 2	Mod 1	Unit 1+2	Silver	Core	Core	23
4	Estimating	Mod 1	Unit 9	Silver	Core	Core	33
5	Patterns	Mod 1	Unit 10	Silver	Core	Core	40
6	Shapes 1	Mod 1	Unit 7	Bronze	Core	Core	46
7	Shapes 2	Mod 1	Unit 7	Silver	Core	Core	50
8	Directions	Mod 1	Unit 8	Bronze	Core	Core	56
9	Units 1	Mod 1	Unit 9	Bronze	Core	Core	64
10	Graphs and Tables 1	Mod 1	Unit 6	Silver	Core	Core	71
11	Place Value 2	Mod 2	Unit 1+2	Gold	Ext	Core	81
12	Rounding	Mod 2	Unit 1+2	Silver	Core	Core	87
13	Number Crunching 3	Mod 2	Unit 1+2	Gold	Ext	Core	93
14	Number Crunching 4	Mod 2	Unit 1+2	Gold	Ext	Core	101
15	Decimals 1	Mod 2	Unit 9	Silver	Core	Core	107
16	Money	Mod 2	Unit 3	Silver	Core	Core	114
17	Negative Numbers	Mod 2	Unit 1+2	Gold	Core	Core	123
18	Number Machines	Mod 2	Ext	Silver	Ext	Core	129
19	Symmetry 1	Mod 2	Unit 7	Silver	Core	Core	136
20	Symmetry 2	Mod 2	Unit 7	Ext	Core	Ext	143
21	Angles	A–B Mod 2 C–G Ext	Unit 8	Gold	Ext	Core	151
22	Units 2	Mod 2	Unit 11	Gold	Ext	Ext	157
23	Decimals 2	Mod 2	Unit 9	Gold	Ext	Core	165
24	Time 1	Mod 2	Unit 4+5	Bronze	Core	Core	175
25	Graphs and Tables 2	Mod 2	Unit 4+5+6	Gold	Ext	Core	184
26	Chance	Mod 2	Ext	Silver	Core	Ext	191
27	Multiply 10, Divide 10	Mod 3	Ext	Gold	Ext	Core	196
28	Fractions	Mod 3	Unit 3	Gold	Ext	Core	203
29	Percentages	Mod 3	Unit 3	Gold	Ext	Ext	212
30	Finding Rules	Mod 3	Unit 10	Gold	Ext	Ext	219
31	Backwards Calculations	Mod 3	Unit 10	Gold	Ext	Ext	229
32	Formulas	Mod 3	Unit 11	Gold	Ext	Ext	234
33	Co-ordinates	Mod 3	Unit 8	Gold	Ext	Ext	242
34	Filling space	A–J Mod 3 K Ext	Ext	Gold	Ext	Ext	248
35	Time 2	Mod 3	Unit 4+5	Gold	Ext	Core	259
36	Averages	Mod 3	Unit 6	Gold	Ext	Ext	267

Ext = Extension

Place Value 1

This chapter is about using thousands, hundreds, tens and units in lots of different ways.

Useful information

a

1 → one	10 → ten	1000 → thousand
2 → two	20 → twenty	
3 → three	30 → thirty	
4 → four	40 → forty	
5 → five	50 → fifty	
6 → six	60 → sixty	
7 → seven	70 → seventy	
8 → eight	80 → eighty	
9 → nine	90 → ninety	
	100 → hundred	

b   100 = 10 tens = 1 hundred + 0 tens
120 = 12 tens = 1 hundred + 2 tens
150 = 15 tens = 1 hundred + 5 tens
1000 = 10 hundreds = 100 tens

c

thousands	hundreds	tens	units	
1	3	5	6	→ this number is one thousand, three hundred and fifty-six

d   304 → three hundred and four
240 → two hundred and forty

Hundreds

A Write these numbers in words.
Example 200 ⇒ two hundred

1. 400
2. 600
3. 900
4. 300
5. 500

6. 800
7. 700
8. 100
9. 1000

Write these words in numbers.
Example three hundred ⇒ 300

10. five hundred
11. eight hundred
12. seven hundred

13. nine hundred
14. two hundred

B Change these numbers into tens.
Example one hundred = 10 *tens*

1. 300 = ___ tens
2. four hundred = ___ tens
3. 800 = ___ tens
4. two hundred = ___ tens
5. 600 = ___ tens

C Work out these additions.
· Example 100 + 100 = 200

1. 200 + 200 =
2. 300 + 400 =
3. 500 + 100 =

4. 300 + 500 =
5. 600 + 300 =
6. 100 + 700 =

D Put each of these lists in order, smallest number first.
Example 200, 100, 500, 300 $\Rightarrow$ 100, 200, 300, 500

1 400, 600, 500, 200   3 200, 900, 800, 700
2 900, 100, 400, 700   4 100, 900, 600, 300

E If ▦ = 100 squares, what number is shown in each question.

Example ▦ ▦ $\Rightarrow$ 100 + 100 = 200

1 ▦ ▦ ▦ =

2 ▦ ▦ ▦ ▦ ▦ =

3 ▦ ▦ ▦ ▦ ▦ ▦ ▦ =

4 ▦ ▦ ▦ ▦ =

Hundreds and Tens

F Write these numbers in words.
Example 150 $\Rightarrow$ one hundred and fifty

1 310   6 360
2 420   7 170
3 140   8 280
4 290   9 430
5 510

Write these words in numbers.
Example two hundred and twenty $\Rightarrow$ 220

10 one hundred and seventy   14 five hundred and fifty
11 three hundred and forty   15 two hundred and eighty
12 two hundred and sixty   16 one hundred and ten
13 four hundred and thirty   17 seven hundred and twenty

G Change these numbers into tens.
Example two hundred and ten = **21 tens**

1. 330 = ___ tens
2. 470 = ___ tens
3. one hundred and forty = ___ tens
4. three hundred and ninety = ___ tens
5. 280 = ___ tens
6. 160 = ___ tens

H Work out these additions.
Example 140 + 130 =

$$\begin{array}{r} 140 \\ + 130 \\ \hline 270 \end{array}$$

1. 330 + 140 =
2. 190 + 100 =
3. 210 + 270 =
4. 120 + 270 =
5. 210 + 50 =
6. 120 + 160 =
7. 170 + 110 =
8. 200 + 270 =

I Put each of these lists in order, smallest number first.
Example 170, 140, 130, 180 = 130, 140, 170, 180

1. 210, 290, 260, 280
2. 390, 380, 360, 370
3. 110, 210, 410, 310
4. 180, 240, 160, 210
5. 720, 390, 410, 170
6. 260, 780, 110, 930

J Write these numbers as hundreds and tens.
Example 310 = 3 hundreds, 1 ten

1. 280 = ___ hundreds, ___ tens
2. 420 = ___ hundreds, ___ tens
3. 930 = ___ hundreds, ___ tens
4. 750 = ___ hundreds, ___ tens

K If 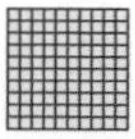 = 100 squares and  = 10 squares, write the number shown by:

Example $\Rightarrow$ 100 + 10 + 10 = 120

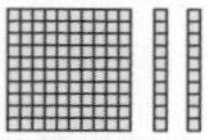

① 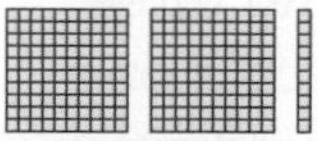 =

② 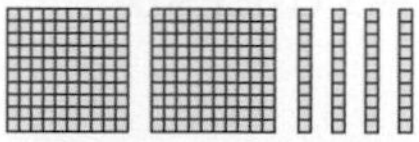 =

③ 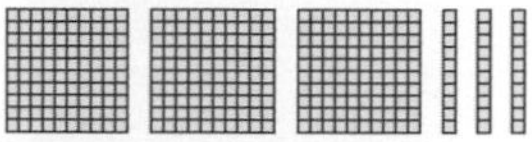 =

④ 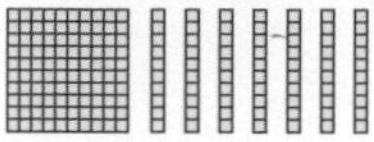 =

If 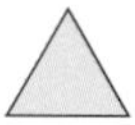 = 100 and = 10, write the number shown by:

Example $\Rightarrow$ 100 + 10 + 10 + 10 = 130

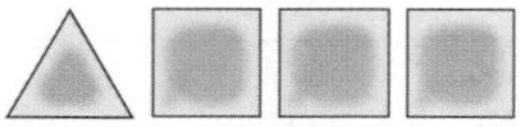

⑤ 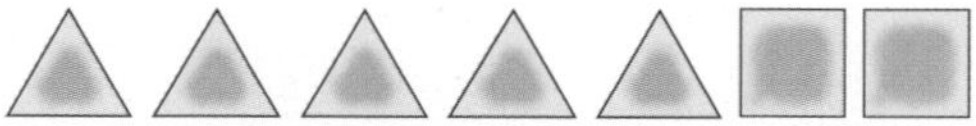 =

⑥ 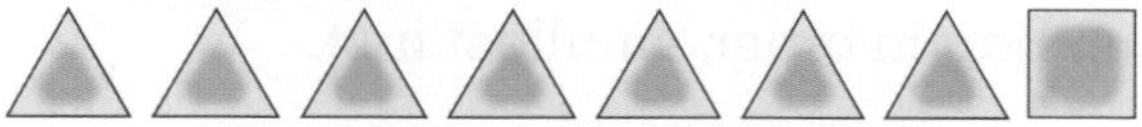 =

⑦ 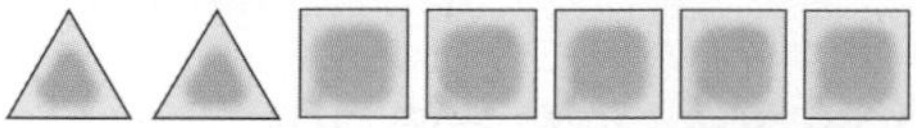 =

⑧  =

Hundreds and Units

L Write these numbers in words.
Example 107 $\Rightarrow$ *one hundred and seven*

① 203
② 304
③ 103
④ 409

⑤ 605
⑥ 702
⑦ 901
⑧ 808

Write these words in numbers.
Example   one hundred and one ⇒ 101

9   three hundred and seven   **14**   five hundred and nine
10   two hundred and four   **15**   four hundred and three
11   nine hundred and two   **16**   seven hundred and one
12   seven hundred and six   **17**   eight hundred and six
13   six hundred and five

M   Work out these additions.

Example   102 + 203 =
$$\begin{array}{r} 102 \\ +\ 203 \\ \hline 305 \end{array}$$

1   404 + 102   **5**   408 + 201
2   502 + 202   **6**   201 + 101
3   709 + 100   **7**   302 + 507
4   307 + 102   **8**   501 + 408

N   Put the numbers in each bag in order, smallest first.

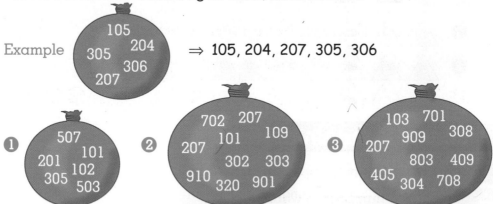

Example   105, 204, 207, 305, 306

1   507, 201, 101, 102, 305, 503

2   702, 207, 101, 109, 207, 302, 303, 910, 320, 901

3   103, 701, 909, 308, 207, 803, 409, 405, 304, 708

O   Write each of these as ___ hundreds and ___ units.
Example   407 = 4 hundreds and 7 units

1   308   **5**   801
2   204   **6**   902
3   903   **7**   107
4   606   **8**   505

P If 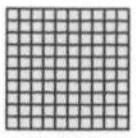 = 100 squares and □ = 1 square, write the number shown by:

Example □ ⇒ 100 + 1 = 101

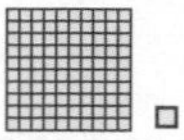

1 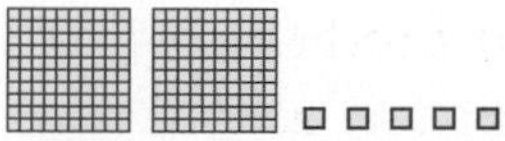 □ □ □ □ □ =

2 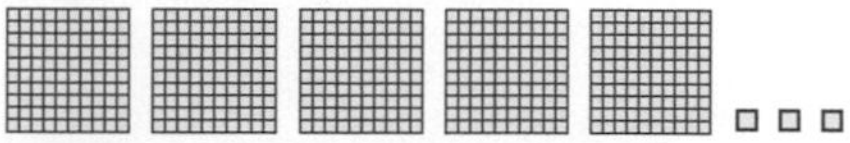 □ □ □ =

3 □ □ □ □ □ □ □ □ =

4 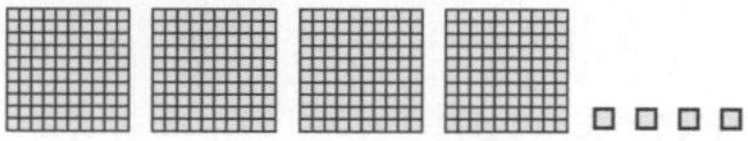 □ □ □ □ =

If △ = 100 units and ◐ = 1 unit, write the number shown by:

Example △ ◐ ◐ ◐ ◐ ⇒ 100 + 4 = 104

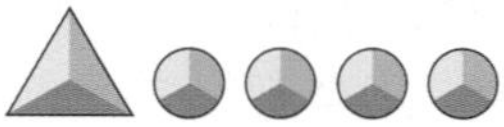

5 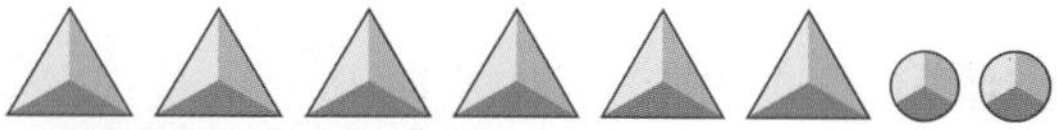 △ △ △ △ △ △ ◐ ◐ =

6 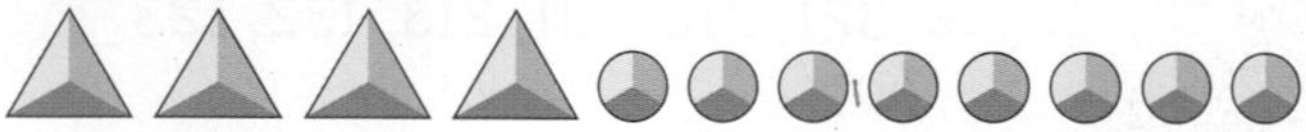 △ △ △ △ ◐ ◐ ◐ ◐ ◐ ◐ ◐ ◐ =

7 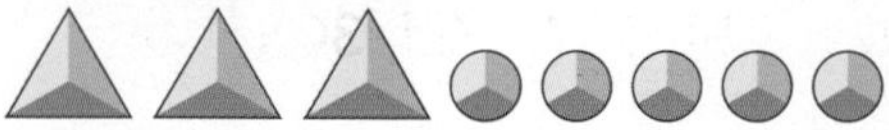 △ △ △ ◐ ◐ ◐ ◐ =

8 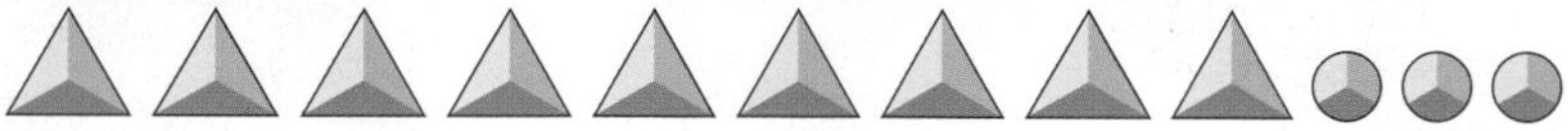 △ △ △ △ △ △ △ △ △ ◐ ◐ ◐ =

Hundreds, Tens and Units

Q Write these numbers in words.
Example 432 ⇒ four hundred and thirty-two

1 274   **5** 627
2 193   **6** 545
3 366   **7** 719
4 298   **8** 989

Write these words in numbers.
Example one hundred and fifty-seven ⇒ 157

9 five hundred and thirty-nine   **12** seven hundred and fifteen
10 eight hundred and sixty-two   **13** six hundred and twelve
11 three hundred and ninety-one

R Work out these additions.

Example 144 + 232 =
$$\begin{array}{r} 144 \\ + 232 \\ \hline 376 \end{array}$$

1 772 + 121   **5** 351 + 146
2 655 + 324   **6** 622 + 314
3 156 + 133   **7** 476 + 123
4 418 + 221   **8** 843 + 152

S Put the numbers in each barrel in order, largest first.

Example
123
132 231
213 321
312

⇒ 321, 312, 231, 213, 132, 123

1
455
554
544
454
545

2
306 236
623 603
632
266
362 336
332 326

3
429 492
499 944
274
922
924 942
742
422

4
192 292
211 199
121
122
219 129
229
291

T Split these numbers into ___ hundreds, ___ tens and ___ units.
Example 276 = 2 hundreds, 7 tens and 6 units

1 425
2 391
3 234
4 488

5 922
6 276
7 648
8 811

U If 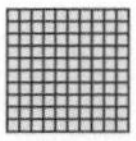 = 100 squares,  = 10 squares and □ = 1 square, write the number shown by:

Example □ □ = 100 + 20 + 2 = 122

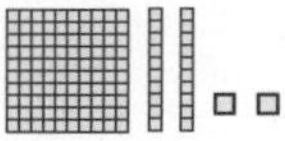

1 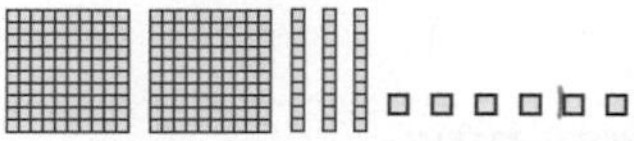 □ □ □ □ □ □ =

2 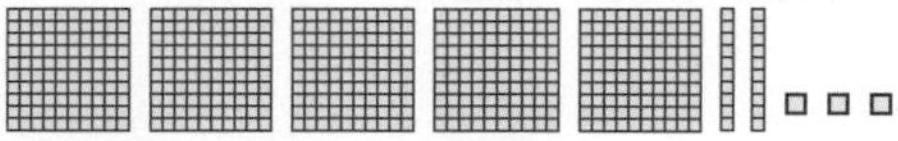 □ □ □ =

3 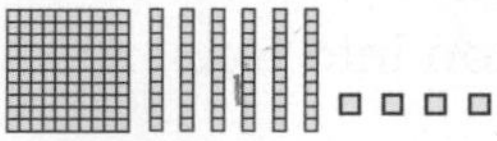 □ □ □ □ =

4 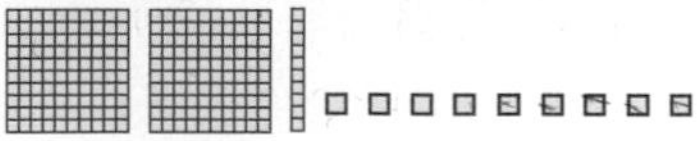 □ □ □ □ □ □ □ □ □ =

V In each question one digit is underlined. Is it the hundreds, tens or units digit?
Example 53<u>2</u> ⇒ units digit

1 <u>4</u>71
2 3<u>9</u>
3 5<u>9</u>3
4 <u>6</u>2
5 60<u>4</u>

6 <u>3</u>99
7 <u>8</u>4
8 40<u>2</u>
9 3<u>0</u>
10 <u>7</u>8

Thousands

W Write these numbers in words.
Example 3000 ⇒ three thousand

1 4000   **4** 6000
2 1100   **5** 3500
3 2000

Write these words in numbers.
Example five thousand ⇒ 5000

6 two thousand, two hundred
7 one thousand and fifty
8 one thousand and seven
9 one thousand, four hundred and twenty-nine

X Change these numbers into hundreds and then into tens.
Example 2000 = 20 hundreds = 200 tens

1 1700 = ___ hundreds = ___ tens
2 1100 = ___ hundreds = ___ tens
3 1500 = ___ hundreds = ___ tens
4 4000 = ___ hundreds = ___ tens

Y Put the numbers in each bag in order, smallest first.

Example 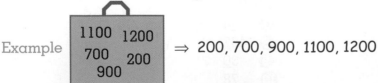 ⇒ 200, 700, 900, 1100, 1200

1

2

3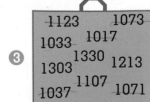

Z Write out each number and underline its thousands digit.
Example 1352 ⇒ 1352

 1476
❷ 2041
❸ 4102

❹ 3331
❺ 5296

✓ Checking your answers

Ask your teacher for the answers to the exercises in this chapter.

How many did you get right?

If any of your answers are not correct, discuss them with your teacher.

? Testing how much you know

When you are finished with this chapter, ask your teacher for the chapter test and see how many questions you can get right.

Remember to write the test score on your student record sheet.

Number Crunching 1

This chapter is about addition and subtraction of one-digit and two-digit numbers. Some of the work may involve carrying or borrowing numbers.

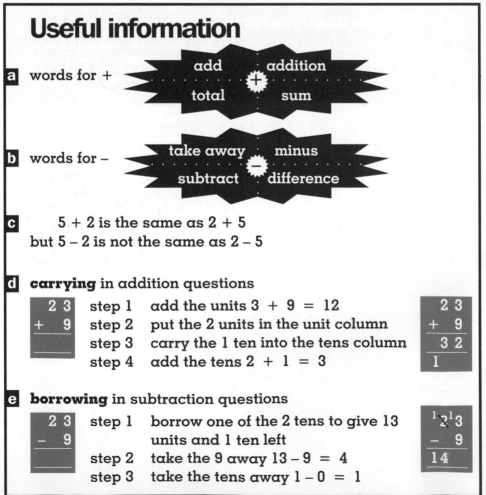

Useful information

a words for +

add · addition

total · sum

b words for −

take away · minus

subtract · difference

c 5 + 2 is the same as 2 + 5
but 5 − 2 is not the same as 2 − 5

d **carrying** in addition questions

$$\begin{array}{r} 2\ 3 \\ +\quad 9 \\ \hline \end{array}$$

step 1   add the units 3 + 9 = 12
step 2   put the 2 units in the unit column
step 3   carry the 1 ten into the tens column
step 4   add the tens 2 + 1 = 3

$$\begin{array}{r} 2\ 3 \\ +\quad 9 \\ \hline 3\ 2 \\ 1 \end{array}$$

e **borrowing** in subtraction questions

$$\begin{array}{r} 2\ 3 \\ -\quad 9 \\ \hline \end{array}$$

step 1   borrow one of the 2 tens to give 13
        units and 1 ten left
step 2   take the 9 away 13 − 9 = 4
step 3   take the tens away 1 − 0 = 1

$$\begin{array}{r} {}^1\!2\,{}^1\!3 \\ -\quad 9 \\ \hline 1\ 4 \end{array}$$

Ch 13 Number Crunchin
Ch 14 Number Crunchin

SUPPORT: S1, S2, S3, S4,
S6, S7

Using Single Numbers

A Find the answer to these additions.
Example 3 + 1 = 4

1 4 + 1
2 3 + 2
3 5 + 1
4 6 + 0
5 5 + 3

6 6 + 2
7 7 + 0
8 5 + 4
9 4 + 4

B Find the two numbers in the panel which give a total of these numbers.
Example 3 = 1 + 2

1 5
2 2
3 1
4 6
5 4

6 12
7 9
8 8
9 10

1 2 0
8 4

Find two joined numbers in the panel which add up to:
Example 4 ⇒ 3•——•1

10 7
11 2
12 6
13 9
14 11

15 12
16 15
17 13
18 14

1•——•5   0•——•2
5•——•8   1•——•3
4•——•3
6•——•9   6•——•3
7•——•5   7•——•7
6•——•5

C Find the answer to these additions.
Example 0 + 0 = 0

1 3 + 3 =
2 5 + 5 =
3 2 + 2 =
4 4 + 4 =
5 1 + 1 =

6 6 + 6 =
7 8 + 8 =
8 7 + 7 =
9 9 + 9 =

D Find the answer to these subtractions.
Example 2 – 1 = 1

1 3 – 1
2 4 – 2
3 3 – 0
4 5 – 2
5 4 – 3

6 6 – 2
7 8 – 1
8 7 – 4
9 6 – 5

E Find two numbers in the panel, which when you take the smaller from the larger one, give these numbers.
Example 2 = 5 – 3

1 4
2 3
3 5
4 0
5 6

6 7
7 1
8 8
9 9

Find the difference between these numbers.
Example 3 and 1 ⇒ 3 – 1 = 2

10 5 and 2
11 6 and 4
12 8 and 6

13 9 and 3
14 7 and 6

F If each child spends £4, how much does each child have left?
Example Tom £7 ⇒ 7 – 4 = £3

1 Anne £9
2 Jim £8
3 Nick £6
4 Ushma £5
5 David £4

G If 3 pieces of fruit are taken from each box, how many are left?
Example 8 oranges ⇒ 8 – 3 = 5, 5 oranges left

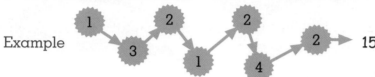

① 6 peaches   **②** 7 bananas   **③** 9 apples   **④** 5 pears

H Look at the chains and find the total of each one.

Example

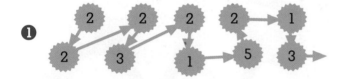

①

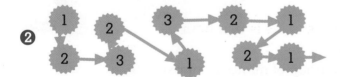

②

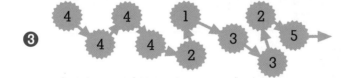

③

④

⑤

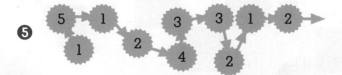

I Follow each route, adding as you go along.

Example

$$\Rightarrow 2 + 3 + 4 + 2 + 1 + 5 = 17$$

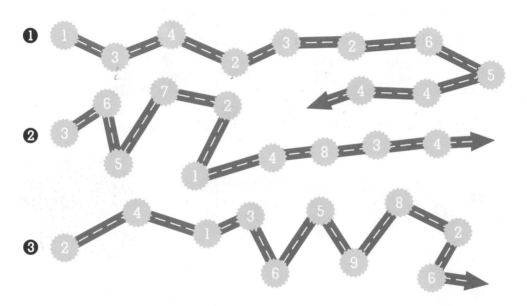

J Find the total in each group of numbered boxes.

Example

1	3
2	5

$\Rightarrow 1 + 3 + 2 + 5 + 1 + 4 + 4 + 1 + 2 + 6 + 2 + 4$
$= 35$

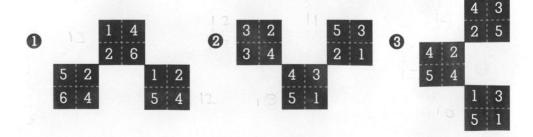

Using Two-digit Numbers

K Find the answer to these additions.
Example $10\,°C + 4\,°C = 14\,°C$

❶ $12\,°C + 5\,°C =$ **❻** $20\,°C + 3\,°C =$
❷ $15\,°C + 3\,°C =$ **❼** $23\,°C + 6\,°C =$
❸ $21\,°C + 6\,°C =$ **❽** $14\,°C + 5\,°C =$
❹ $18\,°C + 1\,°C =$ **❾** $31\,°C + 2\,°C =$
❺ $17\,°C + 0\,°C =$

L Find two numbers in the shape which add up to:
Example $16 = 12 + 4$

❶ 23   **❻** 44
❷ 26   **❼** 35
❸ 14   **❽** 37
❹ 41   **❾** 42
❺ 24

How much money is there in each bag?

Example   £4 £13 $⇒ £4 + £13 = £17$

❿ £7 £21   **⓮** £5 £50

⓫ £8 £20   **⓯** £61 £3

⓬ £5 £33   **⓰** £84 £4

⓭ £2 £44

M Find the answer to these additions.

Example

```
  1 7
+   4
─────
  2 1
  1
```

1
```
  1 5
+   7
─────
```

3
```
  3 6
+   6
─────
```

5
```
  7 7
+   4
─────
```

2
```
  2 8
+   5
─────
```

4
```
  5 9
+   3
─────
```

N By setting out the numbers in each shape in columns, find the total in each shape.

Example 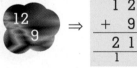 ⇒
```
  1 2
+   9
─────
  2 1
  1
```

1 24 8

5 45 8

2 8 27

6 56 6

3 38 7

7 49 8

4 34 7

8 6 39

O The table shows some people's savings. Work out the total of:
Example Bill + Dave $\Rightarrow$ £12 + £14 = £26

❶ Anne + Nick
❷ Lucy + Mark
❸ Nick + Lucy
❹ Bill + Anne
❺ Dave + Mark
❻ Anne + Mark
❼ Lucy + Anne

Bill	£12
Dave	£14
Anne	£21
Nick	£17
Lucy	£42
Mark	£33

P Find the answer to these additions.
Example

```
  1 7
+ 2 1
  3 8
```

❶
```
  2 3
+ 2 3
─────
```

❸
```
  6 2
+ 2 5
─────
```

❺
```
  4 0
+ 3 6
─────
```

❷
```
  3 4
+ 4 3
─────
```

❹
```
  5 5
+ 3 4
─────
```

Q By setting these numbers out in columns, find the sum of:
Example 25 + 16 =
```
  2 5
+ 1 6
  4 1
  1
```

❶ 37 + 27
❷ 54 + 28

❸ 38 + 25
❹ 66 + 29

R Find the answer to these subtractions.
Example 17 °C – 4 °C = 13 °C

❶ 16 °C – 3 °C =
❷ 25 °C – 4 °C =
❸ 19 °C – 7 °C =
❹ 34 °C – 4 °C =
❺ 56 °C – 5 °C =

❻ 49 °C – 4 °C =
❼ 58 °C – 8 °C =
❽ 38 °C – 7 °C =
❾ 57 °C – 7 °C =

Find two numbers in the panel which have a difference of:
Example 26 = 28 – 2

10 42   **15** 21
11 30   **16** 44
12 24   **17** 33
13 35   **18** 52
14 57

4   28
2   46   7
37   59

S If each person spends £6 how much does each one have left?

Example Tracy ⇒

2	6
–	6
2	0

= £20

1 John   £37

4 Helen £69

2 Anna   £49

3 Andy   £58

Tracy £26

T Find the answer to these subtractions.

Example

$^{0}\not{1}\,^{1}4$
–   5
———
    9

1
1 2
– 7
———

2
2 3
– 5
———

3
3 4
– 8
———

4
4 4
– 7
———

5
5 1
– 4
———

6
2 0
– 4
———

7
3 0
– 5
———

8
5 0
– 7
———

U Find two boxes touching at their corners, which have a difference of:
Example 29 ⇒ 34 – 5

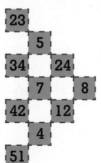

❶ 8
❷ 16
❸ 18
❹ 17
❺ 38
❻ 47
❼ 27

V By setting these numbers out in columns find the difference between:

Example 54 – 21 =
$$\begin{array}{r} 5\ 4 \\ -\ 2\ 1 \\ \hline 3\ 3 \end{array}$$

❶ 45 – 31
❷ 68 – 43
❸ 57 – 26
❹ 73 – 42

❺ 29 – 24
❻ 45 – 42
❼ 57 – 30
❽ 92 – 50

W Use subtraction to find the difference in age between:
Example Colin and Linda ⇒ 48 – 31 = 17

❶ Gill and Ian
❷ Liz and Colin
❸ Duncan and Linda
❹ Paul and Duncan
❺ Paul and Liz
❻ Joan and Ian
❼ Joan and Colin
❽ Colin and Gill
❾ Paul and Linda

Name	Age
Joan	27
Paul	54
Linda	31
Colin	48
Ian	17
Gill	28
Liz	40
Duncan	32

X Find the answer to these subtractions.

Example

$$\begin{array}{r} {}^2\cancel{3}\ {}^1 2 \\ -1\ \ 3 \\ \hline 1\ \ 9 \end{array}$$

❶
$$\begin{array}{r} 3\ 4 \\ -2\ 7 \\ \hline \end{array}$$

❹
$$\begin{array}{r} 5\ 5 \\ -2\ 8 \\ \hline \end{array}$$

❼
$$\begin{array}{r} 8\ 1 \\ -4\ 8 \\ \hline \end{array}$$

❷
$$\begin{array}{r} 3\ 5 \\ -1\ 6 \\ \hline \end{array}$$

❺
$$\begin{array}{r} 4\ 7 \\ -2\ 9 \\ \hline \end{array}$$

❽
$$\begin{array}{r} 9\ 3 \\ -4\ 4 \\ \hline \end{array}$$

❸
$$\begin{array}{r} 4\ 2 \\ -2\ 6 \\ \hline \end{array}$$

❻
$$\begin{array}{r} 6\ 3 \\ -3\ 6 \\ \hline \end{array}$$

Y Find the difference between the two numbers in the shapes by setting the numbers out in columns.

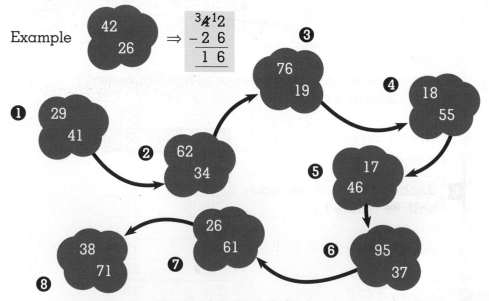

Example
$$42 \quad 26 \quad \Rightarrow \quad \begin{array}{r} {}^3\cancel{4}\ {}^1 2 \\ -2\ 6 \\ \hline 1\ 6 \end{array}$$

❶ 29 41

❷ 62 34

❸ 76 19

❹ 18 55

❺ 17 46

❻ 95 37

❼ 26 61

❽ 38 71

✓ Checking your answers   **Testing how much you know**

Number Crunching 2

This chapter is about multiplying and dividing by 2, 5 and 10.

Useful information

a words for ×

> times   ⊗   multiply
>
> times table   lots of equal groups

b words for ÷

> share equally   ÷   divide
>
> split equally

c double ➡ twice ➡ times 2
half ➡ share by 2

d 2 + 2 + 2 = 2 × 3

e 2 × 3 = 3 × 2
but 10 ÷ 2 is not the same as 2 ÷ 10

f **even numbers** end in 0, 2, 4, 6 or 8

g **odd numbers** end in 1, 3, 5, 7 or 9

13 Number Crunching 3
14 Number Crunching 4

SUPPORT: S8

Using 2s

A If you double the number of each shape in the panel, write down the number of:

Example circles ⇒ 4 doubled = 8

❶ wavy lines
❷ dots
❸ triangles
❹ squares

B Copy and complete the table.

			2 × 3	6
Example	2 + 2 + 2		2 × 3	6
❶	2 + 2		2 ×	
❷	2 + 2 + 2 + 2 + 2		2 × 5	
❸			2 × 6	
❹	2 + 2 + 2 + 2 + 2 + 2 + 2 + 2 + 2		2 ×	
❺	2		2 ×	
❻			2 × 7	
❼	2 + 2 + 2 + 2		2 ×	
❽	2 + 2 + 2 + 2 + 2 + 2 + 2 + 2 + 2 + 2		2 ×	
❾			2 × 8	

C Count in 2s to find the total in each question.

Example  ⇒ 2 + 2 + 2 + 2 = 8

❶

❷

❸

❹

❺

❻

❼

D Copy and complete the table.

Example	$1 \times 2 = 2 \times 1 =$	**2**
①	$2 \times 2 = 2 \times 2 =$	
②	$3 \times 2 = 2 \times 3 =$	
③	$4 \times 2 =$	
④	$5 \times 2 =$	
⑤	$6 \times 2 =$	
⑥	$7 \times 2 =$	
⑦	$8 \times 2 =$	
⑧	$9 \times 2 =$	
⑨	$10 \times 2 =$	

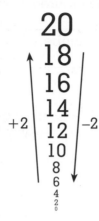

$+2$ $\quad$ 20 18 16 14 12 10 8 6 4 2 0 $\quad$ -2

E John has twice as many of each fruit as Dave.
Copy and complete the table.

	Dave	John
Example	5 apples	10 apples
①	3 oranges	___ oranges
②	8 bananas	___ bananas
③	2 melons	___ melons
④	6 peaches	___ peaches
⑤	7 lemons	___ lemons
⑥	9 pears	___ pears

F On a hundred square, colour all the numbers that are on the $2 \times$ table up to 100.

1	2	3	4	5	6	7	8	9	10
11	12	13	14	15	16	17	18	19	20
21	22	23	24	25	26	27	28	29	30
31	32	33	34	35	36	37	38	39	40
41	42	43	44	45	46	47	48	49	50
51	52	53	54	55	56	57	58	59	60
61	62	63	64	65	66	67	68	69	70
71	72	73	74	75	76	77	78	79	80
81	82	83	84	85	86	87	88	89	90
91	92	93	94	95	96	97	98	99	100

G Copy and complete.
1. All the coloured numbers end in 0, 2, 4, 6 or 8 and are called _____ numbers.
2. All the numbers not coloured end in 1, 3, 5, 7 or 9 and are called _____ numbers.

H Write whether each of these numbers is odd or even.
Example 24 ⇒ *even*

1. 35
2. 17
3. 28
4. 56
5. 92
6. 40
7. 87

8. 63
9. 96
10. 45
11. 30
12. 79
13. 51

I Look at the shapes in the panel. If you get half of each sort, how many is that?
Example squares = half of 8 ⇒ 4

1. wavy lines
2. triangles
3. dots
4. circles
5. lines
6. clouds
7. diamonds

J Share the money in each bag equally into 2 piles.

Example £4 ⇒ £2 + £2

❶ £8   ❻ £12

❷ £6   ❼ £20

❸ £10   ❽ £16

❹ £14   ❾ £18

❺ £2   ❿ £22

K Find the answer to these divisions.
Example 8 ÷ 2 = 4

❶ 6 ÷ 2 =   ❺ 16 ÷ 2 =   ❾ 24 ÷ 2 =
❷ 10 ÷ 2 =   ❻ 14 ÷ 2 =   ❿ 22 ÷ 2 =
❸ 12 ÷ 2 =   ❼ 20 ÷ 2 =
❹ 4 ÷ 2 =   ❽ 18 ÷ 2 =

L Divide these animals into 2 equal groups.

	group 1	animals	group 2
Example	5 cows	← 10 cows →	5 cows
❶		← 12 sheep →	
❷		← 8 pigs →	
❸		← 18 hens →	
❹		← 14 cats →	
❺		← 6 dogs →	

Using 5s

M Count in 5s to find the total number of dots.

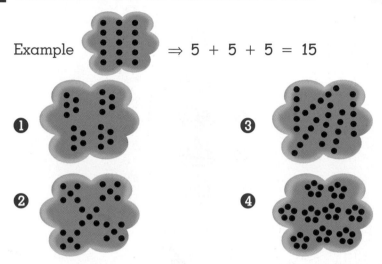

Example ⇒ 5 + 5 + 5 = 15

❶

❸

❷

❹

N Copy and complete the table.

Example	5 + 5		5 × 2	10
❶	5 + 5 + 5		5 × 3	
❷	5 + 5 + 5 + 5		5 ×	
❸	5 + 5 + 5 + 5 + 5 + 5		5 ×	
❹	5 + 5 + 5 + 5 + 5		5 ×	
❺	5 + 5 + 5 + 5 + 5 + 5 + 5 + 5		5 ×	
❻	5 + 5 + 5 + 5 + 5 + 5 + 5		5 ×	
❼	5		5 ×	

O Count in 5s to find out how much money is in each box.

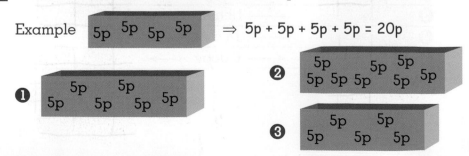

Example 5p 5p 5p 5p ⇒ 5p + 5p + 5p + 5p = 20p

❶ 5p 5p 5p 5p 5p 5p

❷ 5p 5p 5p 5p 5p 5p 5p 5p

❸ 5p 5p 5p 5p 5p

P Copy and complete the table.

Example	$1 \times 5 = 5 \times 1$	5
❶	$2 \times 5 = 5 \times 2$	
❷	$3 \times 5 =$	
❸	$4 \times 5 =$	
❹	$5 \times 5 =$	
❺	$6 \times 5 =$	
❻	$7 \times 5 =$	
❼	$8 \times 5 =$	
❽	$9 \times 5 =$	
❾	$10 \times 5 =$	

$$-5 \quad \begin{matrix} 50 \\ 45 \\ 40 \\ 35 \\ 30 \\ 25 \\ 20 \\ 15 \\ 10 \\ 5 \\ 0 \end{matrix} \quad +5$$

Copy and complete these parts of the $5 \times$ table.

Example | 5 | 10 | | 20 | $\Rightarrow$ 5, 10, 15, 20

❿ | 25 | | | 40 |

⓫ | 10 | | | 25 |

⓬ | | | 35 | |

⓭ | 20 | | | |

⓮ | | | 45 | 50 |

Q Split each of the shapes in the panels into groups of 5 and write down how many small groups are in each panel.

Example 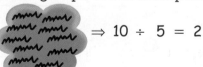 $\Rightarrow$ 10 ÷ 5 = 2

 ❶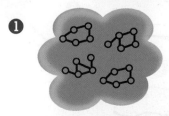

R Share the money in each bag among 5 people. How much will each one get?

Example  £15 ⇒ 15 ÷ 5 = 3

1 £20

2 £35

3 £30

4 £40

5 £25

6 £45

7 £60

8 £55

9 £50

10 £70

S Find the answer to these divisions.
Example 20 ÷ 5 = 4

1 15 ÷ 5
2 30 ÷ 5
3 40 ÷ 5
4 25 ÷ 5

5 35 ÷ 5
6 50 ÷ 5
7 45 ÷ 5
8 60 ÷ 5

9 55 ÷ 5
10 70 ÷ 5

T Divide each of these numbers by 5.

Example 15 ⇒ 15 ÷ 5 = 3

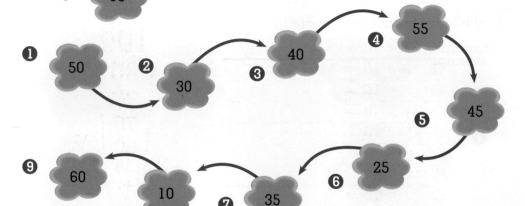

1 50
2 30
3 40
4 55
5 45
6 25
7 35
8 10
9 60

Using 10s

U Count in 10s to find the total number of dots.

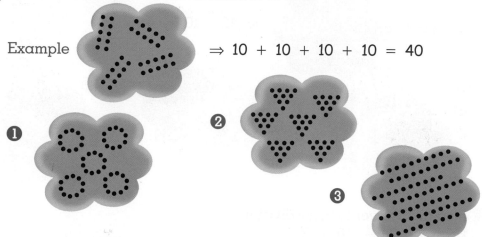

Example ⇒ 10 + 10 + 10 + 10 = 40

❶

❷

❸

V Copy and complete the table.

Example	10 + 10 + 10	10 × 3	30
❶	10 + 10		
❷	10 + 10 + 10 + 10 + 10		
❸	10 + 10 + 10 + 10		
❹	10 + 10 + 10 + 10 + 10 + 10 + 10 + 10 + 10		
❺	10 + 10 + 10 + 10 + 10 + 10 + 10		
❻	10 + 10 + 10 + 10 + 10 + 10		

W Copy and complete the table.

Example	1 × 10 = 10 × 1	10
❶	2 × 10 = 10 × 2	
❷	3 × 10 =	
❸	4 × 10 =	
❹	5 × 10 =	
❺	6 × 10 =	
❻	7 × 10 =	
❼	8 × 10 =	
❽	9 × 10 =	

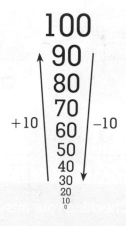

100
90
80
70
60
50
40
30
20
10
0

+10   −10

X How many groups of 10 are there in each panel?

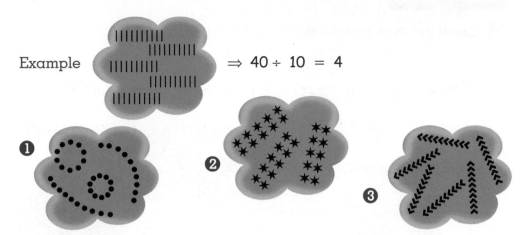

Example ⇒ 40 ÷ 10 = 4

Y Find the answer to these divisions.
Example 20 ÷ 10 = 2

1 50 ÷ 10 =   **5** 80 ÷ 10 =   **9** 90 ÷ 10 =
2 30 ÷ 10 =   **6** 10 ÷ 10 =   **10** 120 ÷ 10 =
3 40 ÷ 10 =   **7** 70 ÷ 10 =
4 60 ÷ 10 =   **8** 100 ÷ 10 =

Z Share each of these sums of money among 10 people. Write down how much money each one gets.

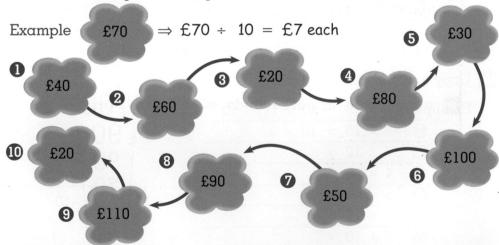

Example £70 ⇒ £70 ÷ 10 = £7 each

Checking your answers   **Testing how much you know**

Estimating

This chapter is about carefully guessing the length, weight or size of various things and then checking by measuring.

Ch 9 Units 1
Ch 22 Units 2

Useful information

a   a fingernail measures about **1 cm**
a big man is nearly **2 m** tall
a bag of sugar weighs **1 kg**

b   we measure length, distance and height in
centimetres (cm), metres (m) and **kilometres (km)**

c   100 cm = 1 m
1000 m = 1 km

d   we measure size or area in **square cm** (cm^2)
or **square m** (m^2)

e   we measure time in **seconds, minutes** and **hours**

f   60 sec = 1 min
60 min = 1 hour

Estimating Length

A   If your little fingernail is about 1 cm wide, copy and complete the table estimating, and then measuring each line with a ruler.

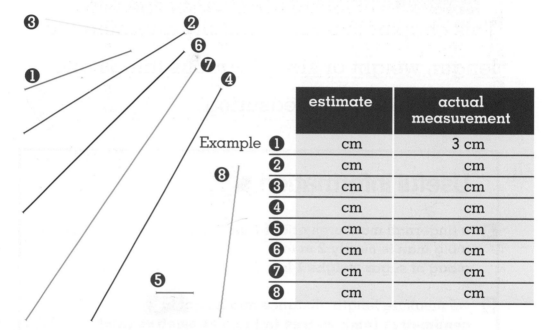

	estimate	actual measurement
Example ❶	cm	3 cm
❷	cm	cm
❸	cm	cm
❹	cm	cm
❺	cm	cm
❻	cm	cm
❼	cm	cm
❽	cm	cm

B   Copy and complete the table, estimating and then measuring each length.

	length	estimate	actual measurement
❶	around your head	cm	cm
❷	your height	cm	cm
❸	length of your desk	cm	cm
❹	your shoe	cm	cm
❺	around your waist	cm	cm
❻	your hand span	cm	cm
❼	your pencil case	cm	cm
❽	your pen	cm	cm
❾	around your wrist	cm	cm
❿	your arm	cm	cm

C If a very tall man is nearly 2 metres high, copy and complete the table, estimating and then measuring each length.

length	estimate	actual measurement
❶ height of your room	m	m
❷ height of the door	m	m
❸ length of the room	m	m
❹ all the way round the room	m	m
❺ the height of your desk	m	m

D Estimate each of these lengths (in m or cm).
Example length of car (m) ⟹ 3 or 4 m

❶ height of a tree (m)
❷ length of a dog (cm)
❸ distance around your school (m)
❹ height of this book (cm)

E Look at the map and estimate the distance from London to these cities.
Example Southampton ⟹ about 100 km

❶ Exeter
❷ Bristol
❸ Swansea
❹ York
❺ Newcastle
❻ Norwich

where | 100 km   200 km   300 km |

Newcastle
York
Birmingham
Norwich
160 km
Swansea
Bristol
London
Exeter
Southampton

Estimating Weight and Size

F If a bag of sugar weighs 1 kg then estimate the weight of:
Example a 2-litre bottle of lemonade ⇒ 2 kg

1 a man
2 a car
3 a lorry
4 a 1-lb box of sweets

G If ▢ is 1 square cm, estimate the surface size of each of these
shapes.

Example ⇒ 4 square cm

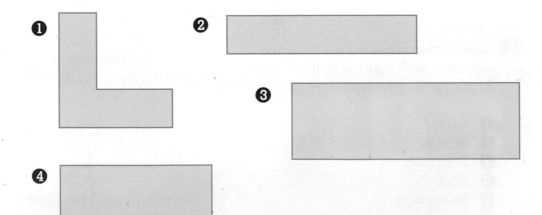

H Now try estimating the surface size of these shapes in square centimetres.

Example  ⇒ about 1 square cm

❶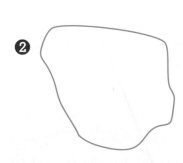

❸

❷

❹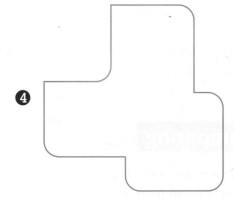

Estimating Time

I Copy the table. Estimate, and then measure the time taken for each one of the tasks.

	task	estimate	actual time
❶	count to 100	sec	sec
❷	write your name and address	sec	sec
❸	blink 50 times	sec	sec
❹	write the numbers 1–50	sec	sec
❺	tap your foot 100 times	sec	sec
❻	work out 50 + 40 + 30 + 20	sec	sec
❼	draw 20 circles	sec	sec
❽	draw a line exactly 30 cm	sec	sec
❾	work out 175–89	sec	sec
❿	count backwards 50–1	sec	sec

J If a woman can walk 6 km in about an hour, work out roughly how long it will take her to walk these distances.
Example 12 km = 6 km + 6 km ⇒ about 2 hours

❶ 18 km   **❸** 2 km
❷ 3 km   **❹** 30 km

K If a runner completes about 10 km each hour, work out roughly how far he will go in these times.
Example 2 hours ⇒ 10 km + 10 km = 20 km

❶ $\frac{1}{2}$ hour   **❸** 3 hours
❷ $\frac{1}{4}$ hour   **❹** $1\frac{1}{2}$ hours

Comparing

L The man in each picture is 2 m high. Estimate the height of each of the things next to him.

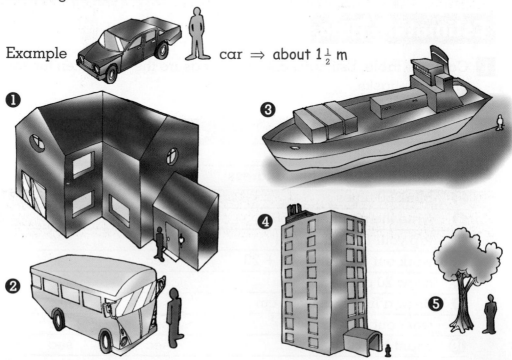

Example   car ⇒ about $1\frac{1}{2}$ m

❶

❸

❷

❹

❺

M If the mug is 10 cm high, how high is each of the other things on the shelf?

Example cereal box $\Rightarrow$ about 20 cm

❶ chocolates   ❸ book
❷ spaghetti jar   ❹ rack

❺ List the objects on the shelf in order, shortest first.

Checking your answers   **Testing how much you know**

Patterns

This chapter is about patterns in calculations, shapes and in lists of numbers.

Useful information

a some patterns repeat what has gone before

e.g.

b some patterns work by following a simple addition or subtraction rule

e.g. | 1 | 3 | 5 | 7 | 9 | 11 | 13 | 15 | **Rule ⇒ + 2**

c some patterns work by following a simple multiplication or division rule

e.g. | 3 | 6 | 12 | 24 | 48 | 96 | 192 | 384 | **Rule ⇒ × 2**

Ch 2 Number Crunchin

Ch 3 Number Crunchin

Ch 18 Number Machin

Ch 30 Finding Rules

Ch 31 Backwards Calcula

Ch 32 Formulas

EXTENSION: E2

Patterns in Multiplication Tables

A Use the numbers in the panel to find the answers to each question.

1 All numbers in the 5 × table end in 0 or 5. Find those in the panel.

2 All numbers in the 10 × table end in 0. Find those in the panel.

3 All even numbers are in the 2 × table. Find those in the panel.

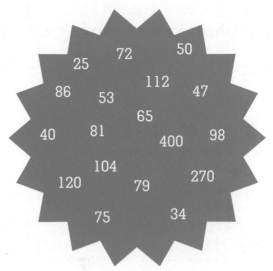

25 72 50 86 53 112 47 65 40 81 400 98 104 120 79 270 75 34

B In the 9 × table the 10s digit goes up 1 and the units digit goes down 1 each time. Complete this list up to 90.

$$18$$
$$+ 1 \; \blacktriangledown \; 27 \; \blacktriangledown \; -1$$
$$36$$

C In the 3 × table the digits must add up to a number in the 3 × table.
Example 123 ⇒ 1 + 2 + 3 = 6 so 123 is in the 3 × table because 6 is too

Which of the numbers in the panel are in the 3 × table?

31 42 114 60 72 76 44 82 102 54

Patterns in Number and Money

D Finish each of the patterns.

1
14 = 10 + 4 or 20 – 6
15 = 10 + 5 or 20 – 5
16 =   or
17 =   or
18 =   or
19 =   or

1
79 = 70 + 9 or 80 – 1
78 = 70 + 8 or 80 – 2
77 =   or
76 =   or
75 =   or
74 =   or

2
51 = 50 + 1 or 60 – 9
52 = 50 + 2 or 60 – 8
53 =   or
54 =   or
55 =   or
56 =   or

4
127 = 120 + 7 or 130 – 3
126 = 120 + 6 or 130 – 4
125 =   or
124 =   or
123 =   or
122 =   or

E These patterns show money in pence. Continue each of the patterns showing which coins are needed to make the total.
Example 20p = 20p
21p = 20p + 1p
22p = 20p + 2p
23p = 20p + 2p + 1p
24p = 20p + 2p + 2p
25p = 20p + 5p

1
30p = 20p + 10p
31p =
32p =
33p =
34p =
35p =

3
80p = 50p + 20p + 10p
81p =
82p =
83p =
84p =
85p =

2
50p = 50p
51p =
52p =
53p =
54p =
55p =

Repeating Patterns

F Copy and continue each pattern.

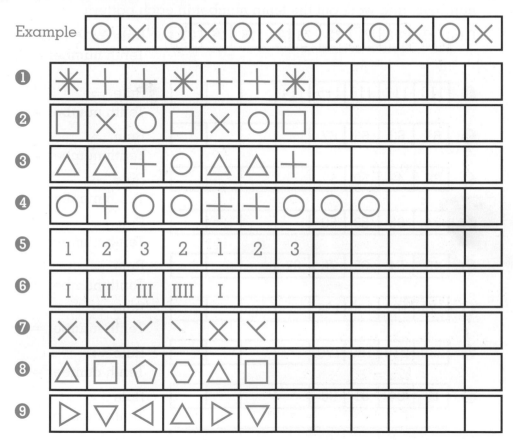

Example ○ ✕ ○ ✕ ○ ✕ ○ ✕ ○ ✕ ○ ✕

❶ ✳ + + ✳ + + ✳

❷ □ ✕ ○ □ ✕ ○ □

❸ △ △ + ○ △ △ +

❹ ○ + ○ ○ + + ○ ○ ○

❺ 1 2 3 2 1 2 3

❻ I II III IIII I

❼ ✕ ＼ ＞ ＼ ✕ ＼

❽ △ □ ⬠ ⬡ △ □

❾ ▷ ▽ ◁ △ ▷ ▽

G Now continue these patterns.

❶

❷

❸

❹

Rules in Number Patterns

H Copy and continue each pattern, give the rule connecting the numbers, and work out the tenth number in each pattern.

Example | 70 | 71 | 72 | 73 | 74 | 75 | 76 | 77 | Rule ⇒ +1 each time
Tenth number = 79

1 | 118 | 117 | 116 | 115 | 114 | | | | Rule ⇒
Tenth number =

2 | 61 | 63 | 65 | 67 | | | | Rule ⇒
Tenth number =

3 | 36 | 43 | 50 | 57 | | | | Rule ⇒
Tenth number =

4 | 74 | 66 | 58 | 50 | | | | Rule ⇒
Tenth number =

5 | 43 | 54 | 65 | 76 | 87 | | | | Rule ⇒
Tenth number =

6 | 174 | 162 | 150 | 138 | | | | Rule ⇒
Tenth number =

7 | 230 | 210 | 190 | 170 | | | | Rule ⇒
Tenth number =

8 | 17 | 34 | 51 | 68 | | | | Rule ⇒
Tenth number =

9 | 150 | 135 | 120 | 105 | 90 | | | | Rule ⇒
Tenth number =

I In these patterns, some parts are missing, but the rule is given. Find the missing numbers and work out the tenth number in each pattern.

1 | 25 | 34 | | | | | | 88 | Rule ⇒ + 9
Tenth number =

2 | | 87 | 81 | | | 63 | | | Rule ⇒ − 6
Tenth number =

3 | | | 101 | | 127 | 140 | | | Rule ⇒ + 13
Tenth number =

J In this question the rule uses × and ÷ . Using a calculator to help, find the missing numbers, the rule connecting them and the tenth number in the pattern.

Example	1	2	4	8	16			

Rule ⇒ × 2
Tenth number = 512

1	3	6	12	24	48			

Rule ⇒
Tenth number =

2	5	10	20	40	80			

Rule ⇒
Tenth number =

3	7	14	28	56	112			

Rule ⇒
Tenth number =

4	1408	704	352	176	88			

Rule ⇒
Tenth number =

5		512	256	128	64	32		

Rule ⇒
Tenth number =

6	2		8	16	32			256

Rule ⇒
Tenth number =

7	2560	1280	640	320	160			

Rule ⇒
Tenth number =

8	4608	2304	1152	576	288			

Rule ⇒
Tenth number =

9	13		52		208	416	832	

Rule ⇒
Tenth number =

10	$\frac{1}{2}$	$\frac{1}{4}$	$\frac{1}{8}$	$\frac{1}{16}$	$\frac{1}{32}$			

Rule ⇒
Tenth number =

11	1	3	9	27	81			

Rule ⇒
Tenth number =

✓ **Checking your answers**   ? **Testing how much you know**

Shapes 1

This chapter is about two-dimensional (2-D) shapes and three-dimensional (3-D) shapes, their names and how we can sort them into groups.

Useful information

a definitions

a **2-D shape** is any flat shape

a **3-D shape** is any solid shape

a **polygon** is a flat shape with straight sides

a **quadrilateral** is any four-sided shape with straight sides

a **regular polygon** has all its sides and corners the same size

an **irregular polygon** has some sides or angles different size

a **right angle** is a corner like this:

an **isosceles triangle** is a triangle with two equal-length sides

an **equilateral triangle** is a triangle with all three sides of the same length

Ch 7 Shapes 2
Ch 19 Symmetry 1
Ch 20 Symmetry 2
Ch 34 Filling Space

Naming Shapes

A Match the shapes to their name by drawing and labelling each one.

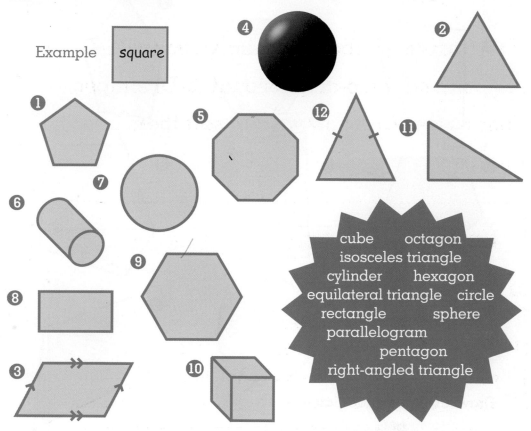

Example   square

cube   octagon
isosceles triangle
cylinder   hexagon
equilateral triangle   circle
rectangle   sphere
parallelogram
pentagon
right-angled triangle

B These shapes can be given more than one name from the list in the panel. Write down those names.

Example   ⇒ square, rectangle, polygon, quadrilateral

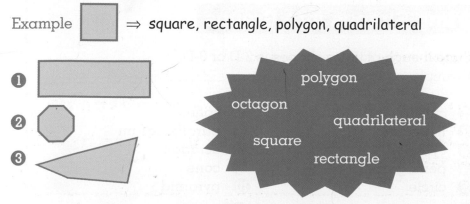

polygon
octagon
quadrilateral
square
rectangle

C Draw each of these shapes and say if it is regular or irregular.

Example [ ] ⇒ regular

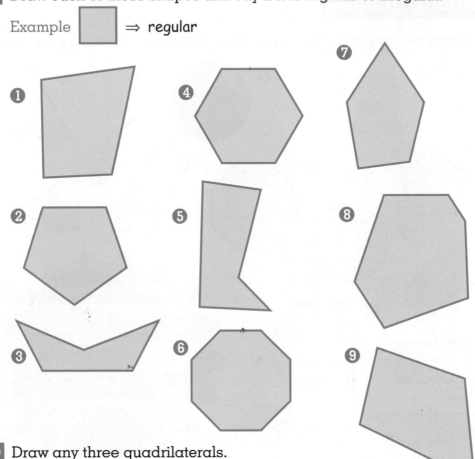

D Draw any three quadrilaterals.

E Draw any three polygons each with more than six sides.

Sorting Shapes into Groups

F State if each of these shapes is 2-D or 3-D.
Example square ⇒ 2-D

1. cube
2. hexagon
3. cylinder
4. pentagon
5. circle
6. sphere
7. parallelogram
8. octagon
9. cone
10. pyramid

G For each question, list the correct shapes from the panel.

Example 3 sides ⇒ c, e, m

❶ straight sides only
❷ curved sides only
❸ 4 straight sides
❹ all sides equal
❺ 5 corners
❻ at least 1 right angle
❼ a mixture of curved and straight sides
❽ 2 sides
❾ 6 straight sides

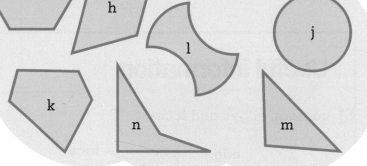

H In which set would you put each shape? Say why you chose that set.

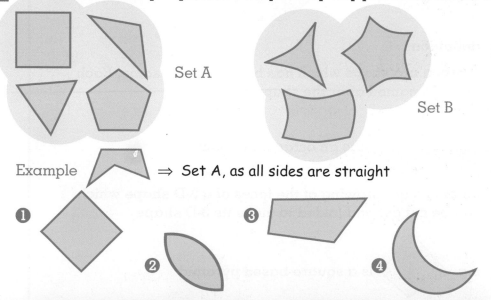

Set A

Set B

Example ⇒ **Set A, as all sides are straight**

❶ ❷ ❸ ❹

✓ **Checking your answers**   ? **Testing how much you know**

Shapes 2

This chapter is about the properties of 2-D and 3-D shapes and the names of some 3-D shapes.

Useful information

a corners, edges and faces

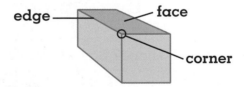
edge — face — corner

b definitions

a **prism** is a shape which has both ends the same. Each prism is named after the shape of its ends

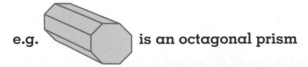
e.g. is an octagonal prism

a **net** is a flat drawing of the faces of a 3-D shape which can be cut out and folded to make its 3-D shape

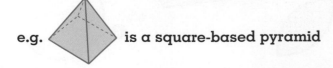
e.g. is a square-based pyramid

a **pyramid** is a flat–based shape which rises to a point

Ch 6 Shapes 1

Ch 19 Symmetry 1
Ch 20 Symmetry 2
Ch 34 Filling Space

WORKSHEET: W1, W2

2-D Shapes

A Using worksheet (1) write down how many sides and corners each shape has.

Example  ⇒ <u>5</u> corners
<u>5</u> sides

❶ 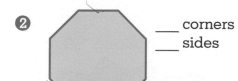 ___ corners
___ sides

❻  ___ corners
___ sides

❷  ___ corners
___ sides

❼  ___ corners
___ sides

❸ ___ corners
___ sides

❽ parallelogram ___ corners
___ sides

❹ 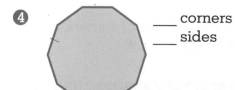 ___ corners
___ sides

❾ ___ corners
___ sides

❺ 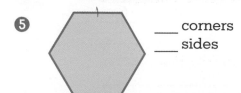 ___ corners
___ sides

3-D Shape Properties

B Using worksheet (2) choose a name from the panel to label
each shape.

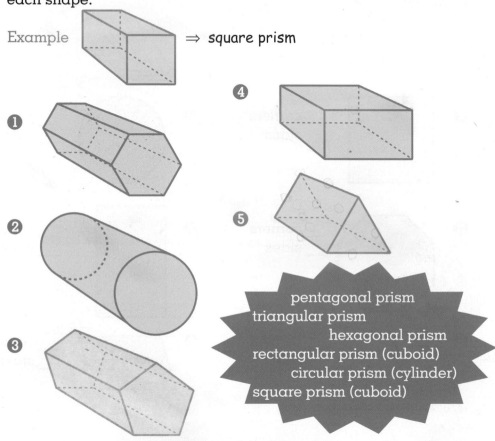

Example   ⇒ square prism

pentagonal prism
triangular prism
hexagonal prism
rectangular prism (cuboid)
circular prism (cylinder)
square prism (cuboid)

C Copy and complete the table to find the number of corners, edges
and faces on each of the six prisms in **B**.

	name	corners	edges	faces
Example	square prism	8	12	6
❶				
❷				
❸				
❹				
❺				

D Look at the diagrams of 3-D shapes. Copy the table and write down the number of corners, edges and faces in each 3-D shape.

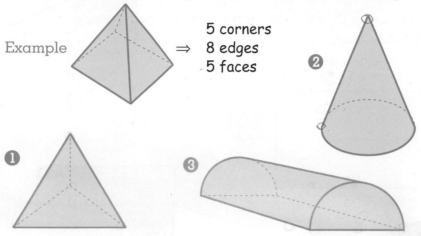

Example ⇒ 5 corners
              8 edges
              5 faces

	name	corners	edges	faces
Example	square–based pyramid	5	8	5
❶	triangular pyramid			
❷	cone			
❸	semicircular prism			

Nets

E Which of these are nets of a cube? Draw the ones that are on squared paper.

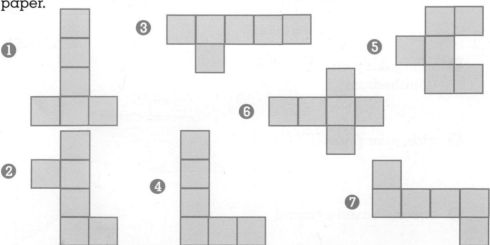

F Match each net to its 3-D shape.

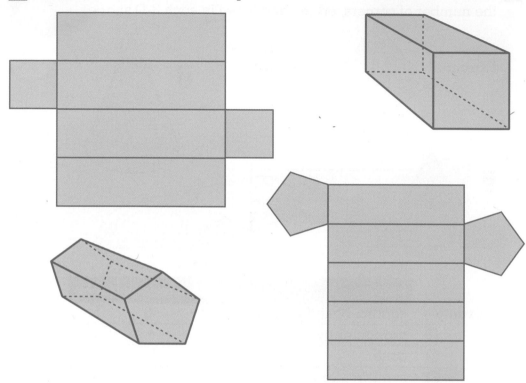

G Draw the net of each of these shapes.

Example ⇒

rectangular prism (cuboid)

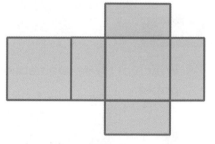

❶ triangular pyramid
   (tetrahedron)

❷ triangular prism

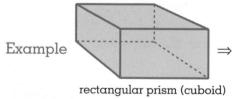

❸ square–based pyramid

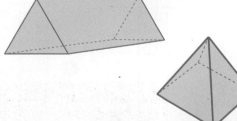

H Which 3-D shapes can be made from these nets?

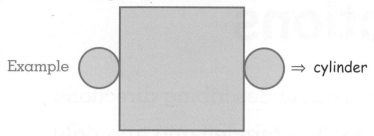

Example 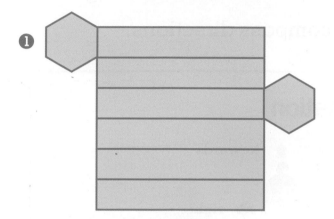 ⇒ cylinder

❶

❷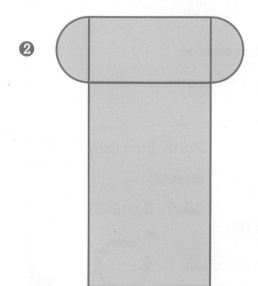

❸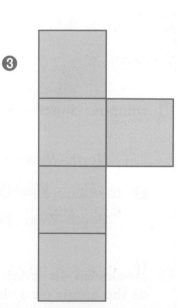

Directions

This chapter is about describing directions using words such as turn left and turn right, and about using compass directions.

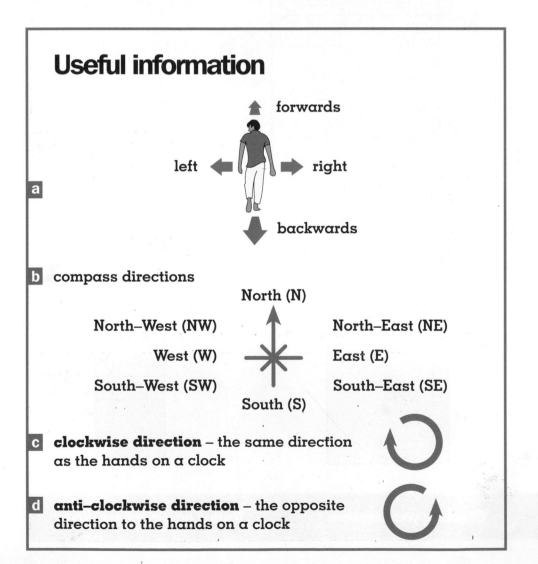

Useful information

a forwards / left / right / backwards

b compass directions

North (N)
North–West (NW) North–East (NE)
West (W) East (E)
South–West (SW) South–East (SE)
South (S)

c **clockwise direction** – the same direction as the hands on a clock

d **anti–clockwise direction** – the opposite direction to the hands on a clock

Ch 21 Angles

EXTENSION: E11

Giving Directions

A Look at the map and give directions using left (L), right (R) and forwards (F).

Example A → B ⇒ F, R, F

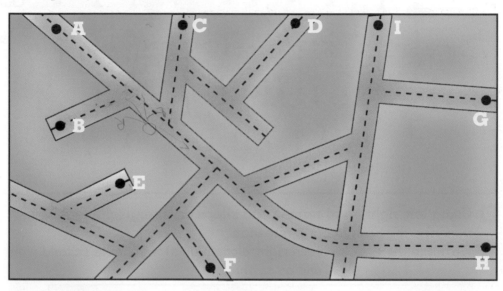

❶	B → C	❻	D → A
❷	C → D	❼	B → E
❸	E → F	❽	F → I
❹	G → H	❾	E → H
❺	H → I		

B Use left, right and forwards to describe the route through the maze.

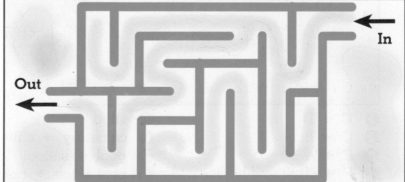

C Using forwards, left and right, find a path through the wood.

D Using left, right, road names and shops or other useful features, describe the path in each question.

Example A ➜ G ⇒ turn right along high street, take second right and go to the end

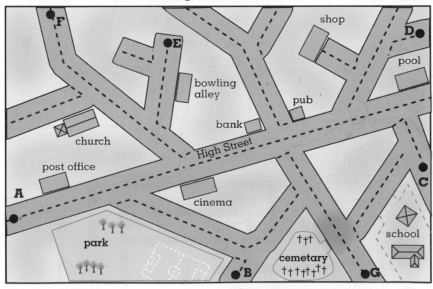

❶ C ➜ D
❷ C ➜ B
❸ E ➜ A
❹ F ➜ C

❺ shop ➜ park
❻ cemetary ➜ church
❼ pool ➜ school
❽ post office ➜ bowling alley

Right-angle Turns

E What letter will the man be facing if he starts by facing A each time and turns through these angles?

Example 1 right angle <u>left</u> → M

1. 1 right angle <u>right</u>
2. 2 right angles
3. 3 right angles <u>right</u>
4. 4 right angles <u>left</u>

F Which number will the hour hand point to if it moves from 12 each time through these angles?

Example 2 right angles → 6

1. 1 right angle
2. 3 right angles
3. 4 right angles
4. 5 right angles
5. 8 right angles

G Which mountain will the woman face if she starts by facing Flat–top Mountain each time and turns through these angles?

Example 1 right angle <u>right</u> → Pointed Mountain

1. 3 right angles <u>left</u>
2. 2 right angles <u>left</u>
3. 3 right angles <u>right</u>
4. 4 right angles <u>right</u>

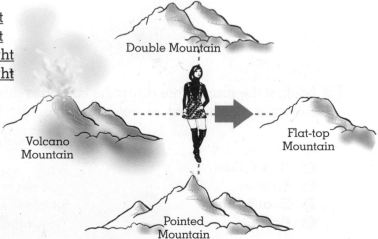

Using a Compass

H Copy and complete the points of the compass and the rules we can use for learning them.

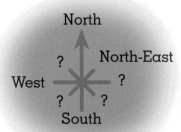

North

? North-East

West ?

? ?

South

<u>N</u>ever <u>E</u>at <u>S</u>hredded <u>W</u>heat

__aughty __lephants __quirt __ater

I Write down the compass direction of each number.
Example 8 ⇒ NW

1 5
2 3
3 4
4 7

North

8 2

7 3

6 4

5

J Write down the compass direction of these letters.
Example G ⇒ SW

1 D
2 H
3 F
4 A

North

H A B

G C

F E D

K Look at the map. Write down the compass direction of each object.
Example North–West ⇒ volcano

1 South
2 North–East
3 West
4 South–East
5 East

treasure chest

North tree

lake

volcano

cross

mountains

L Use two compass directions to describe the routes.

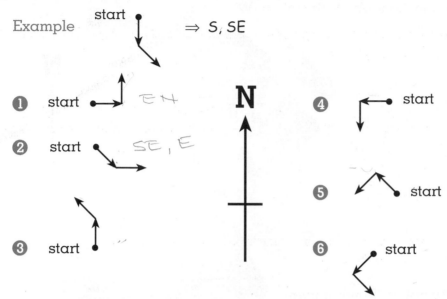

Example   start ⇒ S, SE

① start E H

② start SE, E

③ start

N

④ start

⑤ start

⑥ start

M Start at A and describe the route using compass directions to each of the other letters.
Example A → B ⇒ N, SW, N, W

① A → C
② A → D
③ A → E
④ A → F

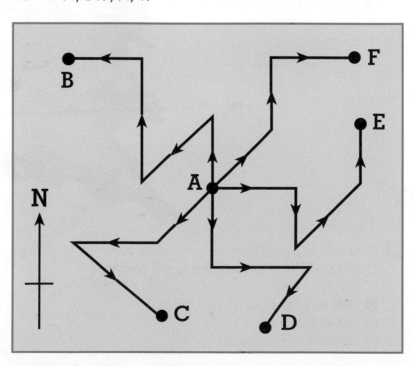

N Give the compass direction between each of the two cities.
Example London → Bristol ⇒ W

1 Bristol → Southampton
2 London → Norwich
3 Glasgow → Edinburgh
4 Newcastle → Southampton
5 Birmingham → Manchester

O Find the city which is:
Example SW of Birmingham ⇒ Swansea

1 NE of Liverpool
2 W of Norwich
3 NW of Birmingham

Clockwise and Anti–clockwise

P Say whether the object is turning clockwise or anti–clockwise.

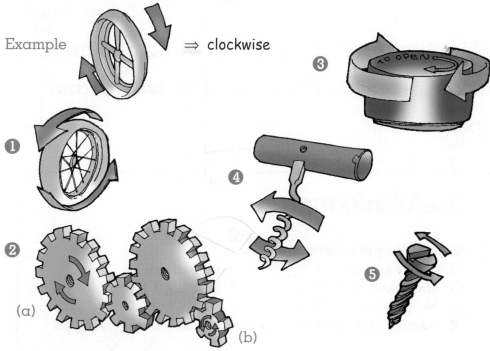

Example ⇒ clockwise

③ TO OPEN

① ④

② ⑤

(a) (b)

Q On this roundabout system say if each car is going clockwise or anti–clockwise.

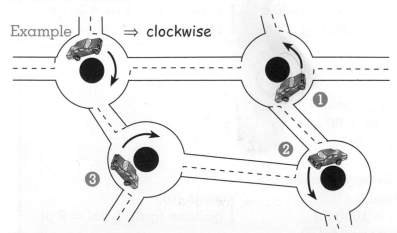

Example ⇒ clockwise

①
②
③

Units 1

This chapter is about using words and units to measure length, distance, time, weight and space.

Useful information

a **units of length or distance** are

millimetres (mm)
centimetres (cm)
metres (m), 1 m = 100 cm
kilometres (km), 1 km = 1000 m

inches (in)
feet (ft), 1 ft = 12 in
yards (yd), 1 yd = 3 ft
miles, 1 mile = 1760 yd

b **units of weight** are

grams (g)
kilograms (kg), 1 kg = 1000 g
tonnes (t), 1 t = 1000 kg

ounces (oz)
pounds (lb), 1 lb = 16 oz
stones (st), 1 st = 14 lb

c **units of time** are

seconds (s)
minutes (min), 1 min = 60 s
hours (hr), 1 hr = 60 min
days, 1 day = 24 hr

d **units of volume/capacity** are

millilitres (ml)
litres (l), 1 l = 1000 ml
cubic centimetres (cm^3),
   1 cm^3 = 1 ml
cubic metres (m),
   1 m^3 = 1000 000 cm^3

pints (pt)
gallons (gal), 1 gal = 8 pt

Ch 4 Estimating

Ch 22 Units 1
Ch 24 Time 1
Ch 34 Filling Space
Ch 35 Time 2

Words We Use

A For each set of pens write down which is the longest and which is the shortest.

Example

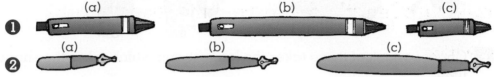

(a)   (b)   (c)

longest ⇒ (a)
shortest ⇒ (b)

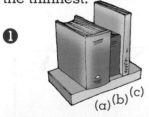

❶ (a)   (b)   (c)

❷ (a)   (b)   (c)

B For each group of people write down who is the tallest and who is the shortest.

Bill   Andy   Jim   Jenny   Alys   Becky

C For each group of books write down which is the fattest and which is the thinnest.

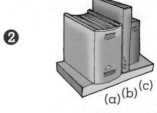

❶ (a)(b)(c)

❷ (a)(b)(c)

D Place all the furniture in order, from narrowest to widest.

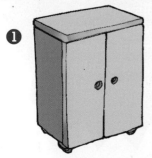

❶

❷

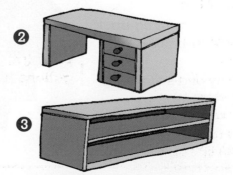

❸

❹

E Choose the lightest and heaviest object from each group.

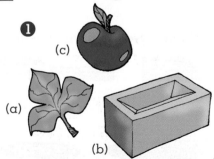

❶ (c) (a) (b)

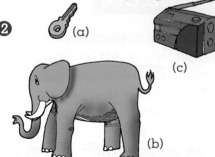

❷ (a) (c) (b)

F Choose which of these takes the longest and which takes the shortest time.

❶ (a) count to 10
   (b) watch a film
   (c) run a marathon

❷ (a) boil a kettle
   (b) blink once
   (c) grow a tree

❸ (a) make a cake
   (b) write your name
   (c) fly to America

❹ (a) eat a biscuit
   (b) drive 60 miles
   (c) do the washing up

G Choose from the panel the piece of equipment you would use to measure:

Example the capacity of a mug ⇒ 1-litre container

❶ the width of this book
❷ the capacity of a small syringe
❸ the weight of a woman
❹ the length of an ant
❺ the weight of a square of chocolate
❻ the length of a running-track
❼ the weight of a pack of biscuits
❽ the capacity of a swimming pool

centimetre ruler
5 ml teaspoon
1-litre container
100 kg weighing scale
millimetre ruler
1 kg weighing scales
metre ruler
a metre cube
spring balance (100 g)

Types of Units

H Choose from the panel the unit you would use to measure:
Example the length of an ant ⇒ millimetres (mm)

❶ the length of a motorway
❷ the length of a classroom
❸ the height of a man
❹ the length of a ruler
❺ the length of your hand
❻ the thickness of a leaf
❼ the distance round the world

millimetres (mm)
centimetres (cm)
metres (m)
kilometres (km)

I Choose from the panel the unit you would use to measure:
Example weight of a chocolate bar ⇒ grams (g)

❶ the weight of a woman
❷ the weight of a lorry
❸ the weight of an ant
❹ the weight of a herd of elephants
❺ the weight of a bag of potatoes
❻ the weight of a house
❼ the weight of an orange

grams (g)
kilograms (kg)
tonnes (t)

J Choose from the panel the unit you would use to measure:
Example a teaspoon of water ⇒ millilitres (ml)

❶ a full tank of petrol
❶ a bath full of water
❸ a can of drink
❹ a glass of milk

millilitres (ml)
litres (l)

K   Choose from the panel the unit you would use to measure:
Example   time taken to run 100 metres $\Rightarrow$ *seconds (s)*

1. the length of a school lesson
2. the time taken to run a marathon (= 26 miles)
3. the time taken to decorate a house
4. the time taken to count from 1 to 10
5. the time taken to cook a chicken
6. the time taken for a tree to grow
7. the time taken to walk a kilometre

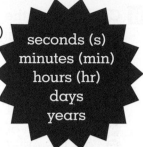

seconds (s)
minutes (min)
hours (hr)
days
years

Numbers and Units

L   Choose from the panel the time that best describes the time taken to:
Example   sprint 100 metres $\Rightarrow$ **13 sec**

1. eat breakfast
2. count from 1 to 10
3. build a house
4. clean your teeth
5. run 1 kilometre
6. count backwards from 100 to 1
7. live a lifetime
8. watch a film
9. drive from London to Edinburgh

5 s
30 s
1 year
70 years
13 s
5 min
2 hours
2 min
10 min
10 hours

M   Choose from the panel the best measure for:
Example   the length of a finger $\Rightarrow$ **9 cm**

1. the length of a classroom
2. the distance round a running–track
3. the thickness of a fingernail
4. the length of a pen
5. a man's height
6. the thickness of an exercise book
7. the length of an arm
8. the distance from London to Birmingham
9. the distance from end to end of a house

170 km
9 cm
70 cm
400 m
2 mm
1 m
15 mm
20 m
13 cm
7 m

N Choose from the panel the best measure for the volume of:
Example a bath full of water ⇒ 85 ℓ

1 a swimming pool full of water
2 a small bottle of cola
3 a large bottle of lemonade
4 a teaspoon full of medicine
5 a can of fizzy drink
6 a tablespoon full of water
7 a duck pond
8 the bathroom sink
9 one drop of rain

360 m³
2000 m³
2 litres
85 litres
10 litres
3 ml
0.1 ml
25 ml
1 litre
330 ml

O Choose from the panel the best measure for the weight of:
Example an elephant ⇒ **2 tonnes**

1 a pen
2 a man
3 a mouse
4 a car
5 a bus
6 a textbook
7 a litre of fruit juice
8 an ant
9 a 2-litre bottle of lemonade

5 g
5 tonnes
1 g
2 kg
70 kg
2 tonnes
200 kg
1 kg
700 kg
75 g

P Put the weights, lengths or capacities of each object in order, smallest
first.
Example 7 cm   70 cm   39 cm   117 cm   27 cm ⇒ **7 cm, 27 cm, 39 cm, 70 cm, 117 cm**

1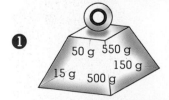
50 g   550 g
15 g   150 g
500 g

3
50 cl
80 cl
180 cl
28 cl
2 cl

2 50 cm   30 cm   170 cm   37 cm   70 cm

4
4 kg   14 kg
240 kg   42 kg
420 kg

Q Put the weights, lengths or capacities in each panel in order, smallest first.

Example 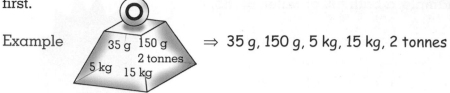 ⇒ 35 g, 150 g, 5 kg, 15 kg, 2 tonnes

❶
| 7 mm | 5 cm | 78 m |
| 7 m | 78 cm | |

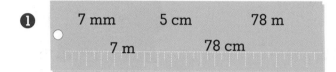

❷ 36 cl
18 l
8 l
800 l
370 cl

❸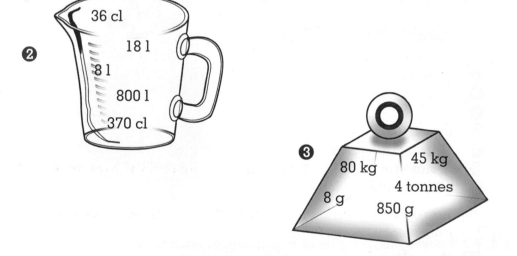
80 kg   45 kg
8 g   4 tonnes
850 g

❹
| 53 cm | 43 m | 4 km |
| 340 m | 35 mm | |

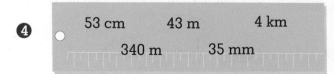

Checking your answers   Testing how much you know

Graphs and Tables 1

This chapter is about drawing tables, charts and pictograms, and answering questions about them.

Useful information

a **tally table** – use lines to show numbers

1 = | 2 = ||

3 = ||| 4 = ||||

5 = ᵀᴴᴸ   6 = ᵀᴴᴸ |

b **frequency tables** – the number of things is shown as a number

c **bar chart** – a block graph with or without gaps between each block

d **Venn diagram**

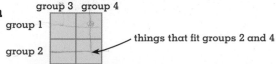

group 1   group 2

things that fit both groups

e **Carroll diagram**

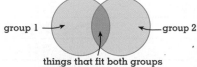

group 3   group 4

group 1

group 2

things that fit groups 2 and 4

f **pictograms** – where information is shown in pictures. Each picture may stand for one or more people or items

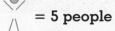

= 1 person   or   = 5 people

Tally Frequency Tables

A Copy and complete the frequency tables by filling in the tallies and frequencies.

❶

Example

favourite drinks	tally	frequency
cola	THL	5
lemonade		3
milk		2
tea		7
coffee		9

❷

types of houses	tally	frequency
terraced		14
semi–detached		12
detached		11
bungalow	THL I	6
other		9

❸

pets owned	tally	frequency
dogs		11
cats	THL III	
rabbits		9
birds	THL THL III	
reptiles	THL I	
mice	THL THL THL	
fish	III	

Bar Charts

B Draw these lines in your book and finish the bar chart for favourite drinks (from **A** **①**).

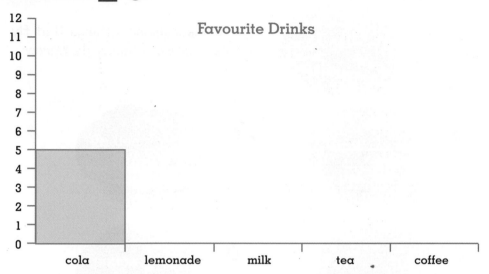

C Draw and complete the bar chart for the types of houses people live in (from **A** **②**).

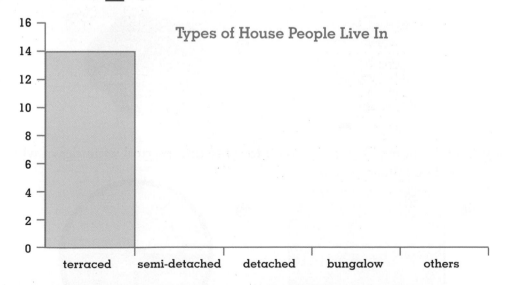

D Draw a bar chart for the results of the pet owners' survey (from **A** **③**).

Sorting into Groups

E Sort the items in each shape into two groups and write down why you chose those groups.

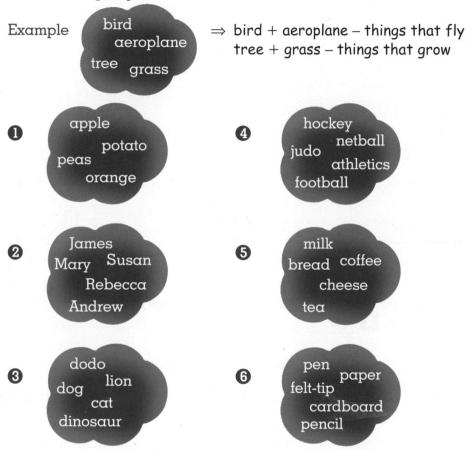

Example

bird
aeroplane
tree   grass

⇒ bird + aeroplane – things that fly
tree + grass – things that grow

❶ apple
potato
peas
orange

❹ hockey
netball
judo
athletics
football

❷ James
Mary   Susan
Rebecca
Andrew

❺ milk
bread   coffee
cheese
tea

❸ dodo
lion
dog
cat
dinosaur

❻ pen
paper
felt-tip
cardboard
pencil

F Sort the items in each shape into three groups and write down why you chose those groups.

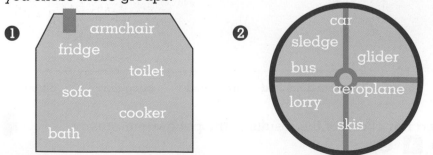

❶ armchair
fridge
toilet
sofa
cooker
bath

❷ car
sledge
glider
bus
aeroplane
lorry
skis

Venn Diagrams

G Copy the circles and put the numbers from the panel onto the diagram.

Numbers
below 10

Even
numbers

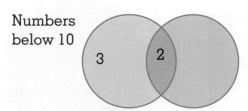

H Copy the diagram and put the words from the panel onto the diagram.

Girls'
names

Names
with an E
in them

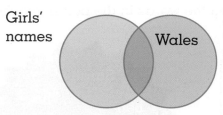

I Copy the diagram and put the words in the panel onto the diagram.

Birds

Things
that fly

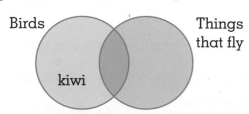

Carroll Diagrams

J Copy and complete the table, putting the numbers in the panel into the correct box.

	numbers 1–10	numbers 11–20
even numbers	8	
odd numbers		

K Copy and complete the table, putting the words in the panel into the correct box.

	beginning with A–M	beginning with N–Z
boys' names		
girls' names		Sarah

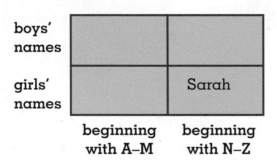

L Copy and complete the table, putting the words in the panel into the correct box.

	fruit	vegetable
red		
orange/yellow		swede
blue/purple		

Finding Information

M Use the table to answer the questions below.
Example list all the males ⇒ Adam Ellis, Alex Tate

name	age	sex	eye colour	hair colour
Adam Ellis	16	Male	Blue	Blond
Mary Parry	27	Female	Brown	Brown
Alex Tate	13	Male	Brown	Black
Anne Malt	19	Female	Hazel	Brown
Lucy Smith	22	Female	Brown	Red

1 List all the teenagers (aged 13–19)
2 List all those with brown eyes
3 Find what colour hair Alex has
4 Find who is 22 years old
5 Find who is the oldest female

N Use the table to answer the questions below.
Example Who came top in Science? ⇒ Sue Mann

name	Maths	English	French	Science	RE	Music	Art
John Tanner	72	77	60	55	61	40	73
Angela Bell	80	51	35	64	71	69	58
Sue Mann	54	67	49	76	37	68	64
Paul Lewis	47	70	30	64	57	82	42

1 Which two pupils had the same mark in Science?
2 What was Paul's worst mark?
3 In which exams did Angela come top?
4 Who found Art most difficult?
5 In which exam did John get his best mark?
6 Who had double Paul's mark in French?
7 Who scored 37 in RE?

O This is a bar chart of average sunshine during a year. Answer the questions below.

Example Which month had most sunshine? ⇒ September

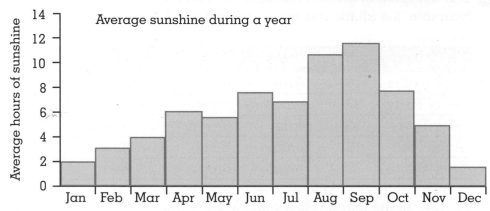

1 Which month had 6 hours of sunshine?
2 How much sunshine was there in November?
3 Which month had more sunshine, June or July?
4 Which month had least sunshine?

P This is a bar chart of an office clerk's working time. Answer the questions below.

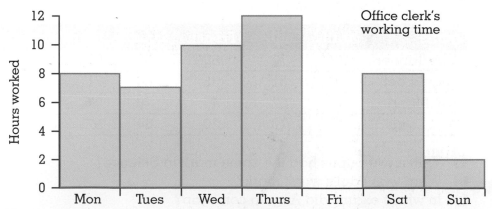

1 On which two days did the clerk work the same number of hours?
2 How many hours did the clerk work on Wednesday?
3 On which day did the clerk work the longest hours?
4 Which day did the clerk take as holiday?
5 How many hours did the clerk work over the weekend?
6 How many hours did the clerk work during the whole week?

Pictograms

Q This is a pictogram of the letters delivered by a postwoman over a period of one week. Answer the questions below.

day of the week	number of letters delivered
Monday	✉ ✉ ✉ ✉ ✉
Tuesday	✉ ✉
Wednesday	✉ ✉ ✉
Thursday	✉
Friday	✉ ✉ ✉ ✉ ✉ ✉
Saturday	✉

key
✉ = 10 letters

Write down how many letters were delivered:
Example on Monday ⇒ *50 letters*

❶ on Wednesday
❷ on Friday
❸ in the whole week

R This is a pictogram of the apples picked by a farmer over 5 days. Answer the questions below.

day of the week	number of apples picked
Monday	🍎 🍎 🍎
Tuesday	🍎 🍎 🍎 🍎 🍎
Wednesday	🍎 🍎
Thursday	🍎 🍎 🍎 🍎 🍎 🍎
Friday	🍎 🍎 🍎 🍎

key 🍎 = 100 apples

Write down how many apples were picked:
Example on Wednesday ⇒ *200 apples*

❶ on Tuesday
❷ on Thursday
❸ on Friday
❹ in the whole 5 days

S Draw a pictogram for each of these frequency tables.
How people get to school

	transport	number	pictogram		
Example	car	10	人人人人人人人人人人	key	人 = 1 person
	bus	3	人人人		
	walk	8	人人人人人人人人		
	cycle	2	人人		

❶ Favourite places to go

favourite places	number
cinema	8
shops	10
restaurant	16
disco	14
theatre	7

key 人 = 2 people
　　 ⸠ = 1 person

e.g. 人⸠ = 3 people

❷ Favourite meals

favourite food	number
Indian	13
Chinese	5
fish and chips	8
burgers	11
steak	9

key ✗ = 2 people
　　 ╲ = 1 person

e.g. ✗╲ = 3 people

❸ Visitors to a restaurant

day of the week	number
Monday	30
Tuesday	20
Wednesday	15
Thursday	25
Friday	22
Saturday	26
Sunday	21

key = 5 visitors
　　 = 4 visitors
　　 = 3 visitors
　　 = 2 visitors
　　 = 1 visitor

e.g. = 12 people

✓ Checking your answers　　　**● Testing how much you know**

Place Value 2

This chapter is about understanding thousands and millions, and writing them in words and numbers.

Useful information

a   1000 → one thousand   500 → $\frac{1}{2}$ thousand

10 000 → ten thousand   250 → $\frac{1}{4}$ thousand

100 000 → one hundred thousand   750 → $\frac{3}{4}$ thousand

1 000 000 → one million

b $\frac{1}{4}$ million → 250 000

$\frac{1}{2}$ million → 500 000

$\frac{3}{4}$ million → 750 000

c   place value

millions	hundred thousands	ten thousands	thousands	hundreds	tens	units
1	7	0	3	2	8	6

1 703 286 → one million, seven hundred and three thousand, two hundred and eighty–six

2 040 099 → two million, forty thousand and ninety–nine

Ch 1 Place Value 1

Ch 12 Rounding

Ch 28 Fractions

Words ←→ Numbers

A Write these numbers in words.
Example 726 ⇒ seven hundred and twenty–six

1 391
2 420
3 690
4 408

5 2891
6 5136
7 2360
8 8420

B Write these numbers in words.
Example 2308 ⇒ two thousand, three hundred and eight

1 9703
2 4091
3 1027
4 4200

5 3020
6 4070
7 9004
8 2007

C Change these words into numbers.
Example three hundred and twenty–four ⇒ 324

1 four hundred and ninety–seven
2 nine hundred and thirty
3 two hundred and seventy
4 five hundred and nine
5 seven hundred and seven
6 two thousand, five hundred and forty–two
7 eight thousand, two hundred and ninety–nine
8 four thousand, nine hundred and thirty
9 six thousand, three hundred and eight
10 three thousand and twenty–four
11 five thousand and seven
12 four thousand and ten
13 ten thousand
14 six thousand, six hundred

D Write each of these newspaper headlines in words.

Example | £12 000 profit | ⇒ twelve thousand pounds profit

1 | £6380 lottery win

2 | 24 000 pens stolen

3 | 2250 injured in Hurricane Bill

E Change these words into numbers.
Example sixty thousand ⇒ 60 000

1 one hundred and twenty thousand
2 forty–seven thousand
3 four hundred and seven thousand
4 one hundred and fifty–three thousand

F If $\frac{1}{2}$ a thousand is 500, write these as numbers only.
Example $1\frac{1}{2}$ thousand ⇒ **1500**

1 $3\frac{1}{2}$ thousand
2 $5\frac{1}{2}$ thousand
3 $8\frac{1}{2}$ thousand
4 $10\frac{1}{2}$ thousand
5 $12\frac{1}{2}$ thousand

6 $17\frac{1}{2}$ thousand
7 $22\frac{1}{2}$ thousand
8 $45\frac{1}{2}$ thousand
9 $57\frac{1}{2}$ thousand

G Copy and complete the table.

	match	number of people at the match	
Example	United v City	$37\frac{1}{2}$ thousand	= 37 500
1	Stars v Colts		= 7 500
2	Town v Rovers	$14\frac{1}{2}$ thousand	=
3	Belles v Ladies	$8\frac{1}{2}$ thousand	=
4	Spartans v Orient		= 11 500
5	Cardinals v Devils		= 52 500
6	Trotters v Redskins		= 77 500

H As 1 000 000 is 1 million, write these numbers in words.
Example 2 000 000 ⇒ 2 million

① 4 000 000
② 7 000 000
③ 9 000 000
④ 13 000 000

⑤ 21 000 000
⑥ 49 000 000
⑦ 57 000 000

I Write each of these in numbers only.
Example 3 million ⇒ 3 000 000

① six million
② ten million
③ 16 million

④ 35 million
⑤ seventy million

J As 500 000 is $\frac{1}{2}$ million, write these as numbers only.
Example $1\frac{1}{2}$ million ⇒ 1 500 000

① $4\frac{1}{4}$ million
② $8\frac{1}{2}$ million
③ $12\frac{1}{2}$ million
④ $\frac{1}{4}$ million

⑤ $\frac{3}{4}$ million
⑥ $3\frac{1}{4}$ million
⑦ $5\frac{3}{4}$ million

K Write each of these newspaper headlines using numbers only.

Example | £10 million win | ⇒ £10 000 000

① | $4\frac{1}{2}$ million out of work |
③ | £20 million missing from bank |
② | £$7\frac{1}{4}$ million bill |

L Make up a newspaper headline for each of these numbers.
Example 4 000 000 ⇒ 4 million unemployed

① 7 500 000
② £10 000 000

③ 2 250 000
④ £8 750 000

Finding Large Numbers

M Use a calculator to work out the answers to the questions.
Write the answers in numbers and words.

Example $\boxed{200 \times 10\ 000}$ ⇒ 2 000 000 = 2 million

① $\boxed{40 \times 500\ 000}$ ⑤ $\boxed{6000 \times 4000}$

② $\boxed{10\ 000\ 000 \div 2}$ ⑥ $\boxed{10\ \text{THOUSAND} \times 500}$

③ $\boxed{130\ 000 \times 50}$ ⑦ $\boxed{25 \times 50\ \text{THOUSAND}}$

④ $\boxed{20\ \text{MILLION} \div 8}$ ⑧ $\boxed{2\frac{1}{2}\ \text{MILLION} + 2\frac{1}{2}\ \text{MILLION}}$

N You need a watch and a calculator to help you in this question.

① Measure your pulse rate for 1 minute
② Work out your pulse rate for 1 hour (60 minutes)
③ Work out your pulse rate for 1 day (24 hours)
④ Work out your pulse rate for 1 year (365 days)

O Use a calculator to work out these questions.

① How many seconds there are in a week
② How many centimetres (cm) in 4 kilometres (km)
③ How many days there are in a century (100 years)
④ How many grams (g) there are in 4 tonnes (t)

Place Value

P Use words from the panel to describe the underlined figure in each question.
Example 54 2̲80 ⇒ 2 hundreds

1. 172̲ 401
2. 4̲ 152 000
3. 17 244 405̲
4. 8 4̲00 092
5. 42 81̲1
6. 5̲7 913
7. 14̲ 211 747
8. 29̲7 411
9. 4̲82 357

units
tens
hundreds
thousands
ten thousands
hundred thousands
millions

Q Use words from the panel in **P** to describe the value of the digit **3** in each of these numbers.
Example 23 481 ⇒ 3 thousand

1. 40 237
2. 137 400
3. 460 463
4. 13 402 294
5. 348 897

6. 76 356
7. 4 107 439
8. 493 028
9. 3 924 695

Checking your answers   **Testing how much you know**

Rounding

This chapter is about rounding numbers to the nearest easy number to use such as the nearest ten or hundred.

Useful information

a rounding to the nearest ten or 10 pence (p)
- if it ends in 5, 6, 7, 8 or 9, round up to the next ten
- if it ends in 0, 1, 2, 3 or 4, stay with the ten that you have

e.g.   77 → 80   46p → 50p   229 → 230
       71 → 70   43p → 40p   222 → 220

b rounding to the nearest hundred
- if the number ends in 50 or more, round up to the next hundred
- if the number ends in less than 50, stay with the hundred that you have

e.g.   170 → 200   2368 → 2400
      110 → 100   2335 → 2300

c rounding to the nearest pound in money (£)
- if the number ends in .50 or more, round up to the nearest £
- if the number ends in less than .50, stay with the £s you have

e.g.   £4.50 → £5.00   £4.40 → £4.00

d rounding to the nearest whole number
- if the number ends in .5 or more, round up to the next whole number, otherwise stay with the number you have

e.g.   6.7 → 7   6.3 → 6

3 Number Crunching 2

13 Number Crunching 3
14 Number Crunching 4
Ch 15 Decimals 1
Ch 16 Money

Rounding to the Nearest Ten

A Round each of these numbers to the nearest ten.
Example 23 ⟹ 20

1 37
2 44
3 91
4 87
5 62

6 49
7 31
8 55
9 84

B Now try the same with these numbers.
Example 119 ⟹ 120

1 223
2 178
3 342
4 811
5 968

6 108
7 324
8 455
9 602

C Round each of these prices to the nearest 10p.

Example 17p ⟹ 20p

1 23p

6 £1.23

2 34p

3 79p

7  £4.79

4 65p

8 £3.28

5 £2.76

9 £2.43

Rounding to the Nearest Hundred

D Round each of these numbers to the nearest hundred.
Example 140 ⇒ 100

① 270
② 310
③ 590
④ 450
⑤ 237

⑥ 781
⑦ 392
⑧ 511
⑨ 647

E Now try the same with these numbers.
Example 1220 ⇒ 1200

① 2180
② 3530
③ 1690
④ 4802
⑤ 1776

⑥ 2229
⑦ 3658
⑧ 7804
⑨ 5924

F Round each of these prices to the nearest £1 (100p).

Example £12.42 ⇒ £12.00

① £14.85
② £7.32
③ £15.39
④ £17.73
⑤ £23.17

⑥ £29.70
⑦ £12.57
⑧ £34.89
⑨ £8.51

G Round each of the attendances at Windy Town FC to the nearest hundred.

	opposition	attendance	rounded
Example	v Albion	772	800
1	v Windy City	845	
2	v Rovers	1082	
3	v Town	4131	
4	v United	2777	
5	v Argyle	899	
6	v Rangers	1490	
7	v Athletic	1702	
8	v Wanderers	3021	
9	v Villa	1850	

H Round the number of visitors to the theme park to the nearest hundred.

	day	visitors	rounded
Example	Monday	3724	3700
1	Tuesday	2941	
2	Wednesday	4307	
3	Thursday	2153	
4	Friday	5348	
5	Saturday	4742	
6	Sunday	6158	

Rounding to the Nearest Whole Number

I Round each of these numbers to the nearest whole number.
Example 4.2 ⇒ 4

1. 3.7
2. 8.9
3. 11.6
4. 15.5
5. 17.4

6. 23.1
7. 10.3
8. 54.9
9. 19.7

J Now try the same with these numbers.
Example 3.91 $\Rightarrow$ **4**

1. 7.26
2. 16.41
3. 19.11
4. 63.78
5. 127.4

6. 319.214
7. 83.72
8. 420.63
9. 111.11

K Work out the answer on a calculator and round it to the nearest whole number.

Example $\boxed{64.5 \div 15}$ = 4.3 $\Rightarrow$ **4**

1. $\boxed{330.2 \div 26}$
2. $\boxed{5.9 + 7.7}$
3. $\boxed{80 - 17.82}$
4. $\boxed{75 - 56.11}$
5. $\boxed{5.8 \times 5.8}$

6. $\boxed{17.3 + 54.1}$
7. $\boxed{27.6 \div 5}$
8. $\boxed{62.5 \times 7.4}$
9. $\boxed{18.48 + 19.32}$

Rounding in Calculations

To give a rough estimate of how much a shopping bill is going to be, the prices can be rounded and added to give a rough total.

L Round both the prices to the nearest 10p, then find the rough total price.
Example 42p + 37p $\Rightarrow$ 40p + 40p $\doteq$ 80p

1. 57p + 49p
2. 44p + 31p
3. 63p + 29p
4. 65p + 45p

5. 191p + 155p
6. 111p + 602p
7. 324p + 178p
8. 455p + 223p

M Round both the prices to the nearest £1 (100p), then find the rough total price.

Example £2.40 + £3.70 ⇒ £2 + £4 = £6

1 £5.92 + £6.85

2 £7.42 + £4.89

3 £3.66 + £8.10

4 £5.51 + £3.46

5 £10.70 + £6.58

6 £12.37 + £9.22

7 £15.75 + £13.99

8 £22.50 + £16.24

✓ **Checking your answers**   ● **Testing how much you know**

Number Crunching 3

This chapter is about addition and subtraction (+ and –) of 3 and 4 digit numbers without the use of a calculator. It is also about multiplying and dividing (× and ÷), using numbers from the times tables without the use of a calculator.

2 Number Crunching 1

14 Number Crunching 4
27 Multiply 10, Divide 10

JPPORT: S9, S10, S11,
2, S13, S14, S15, S16,
S17, S18

Useful information

a   signs   sum   }   =   ✳ **+**   take away   }   =   ✳ **−**
                 add   difference
                 total   left over
                 altogether   more than

                 times   }   =   ✳ **×**   share   }   =   ✳ **÷**
                 multiply   divide
                 lots of   split

b   times tables – remember 4×6 is the same as 6×4
                                  $7 \times 3 = 3 \times 7$
                – choose whichever way you find easier!

c   remember   – in × calculations, you will sometimes need to carry digits to the left

d   remember   – in ÷ calculations, you will sometimes need to carry digits to the right

Addition and Subtraction

A Find the total length of each of the routes from A to B
showing your working.

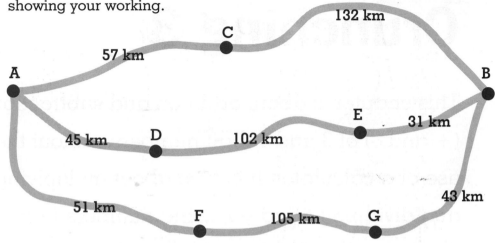

B Copy and complete, showing your working.

Example
```
   132
 + 243
 -----
   375
```

1
```
   316
 +280
 ----
```

5
```
   485
 +116
 ----
```

9
```
   376
 +155
 ----
```

2
```
   591
 +207
 ----
```

6
```
   162
 +254
 ----
```

10
```
   586
 +168
 ----
```

3
```
   247
 +105
 ----
```

7
```
   385
 +444
 ----
```

11
```
   374
 +529
 ----
```

4
```
   363
 +219
 ----
```

8
```
   471
 +277
 ----
```

C If each person listed in the table below spends £132 on a
holiday, how much money do they have left? Copy and complete
the table by setting each one out in columns and showing
your working.

	name	money	money left
Example	Lee	£252	£120
1	Angela	£347	
2	Sue	£535	
3	William	£473	
4	Rachel	£634	
5	Tony	£166	
6	Imran	£395	
7	Ray	£287	
8	Anita	£848	
9	David	£772	

Lee
$$\begin{array}{r} £252 \\ -£132 \\ \hline £120 \end{array}$$

D Copy and complete, showing your working.

Example
$$\begin{array}{r} 458 \\ -146 \\ \hline 312 \end{array}$$

1
$$\begin{array}{r} 375 \\ -262 \\ \hline \end{array}$$

2
$$\begin{array}{r} 841 \\ -310 \\ \hline \end{array}$$

3
$$\begin{array}{r} 373 \\ -119 \\ \hline \end{array}$$

4
$$\begin{array}{r} 824 \\ -307 \\ \hline \end{array}$$

5
$$\begin{array}{r} 268 \\ -159 \\ \hline \end{array}$$

6
$$\begin{array}{r} 327 \\ -155 \\ \hline \end{array}$$

7
$$\begin{array}{r} 856 \\ -392 \\ \hline \end{array}$$

8
$$\begin{array}{r} 477 \\ -285 \\ \hline \end{array}$$

9
$$\begin{array}{r} 523 \\ -199 \\ \hline \end{array}$$

10
$$\begin{array}{r} 647 \\ -198 \\ \hline \end{array}$$

11
$$\begin{array}{r} 811 \\ -376 \\ \hline \end{array}$$

E Find the total weight in each box by setting out the weights in columns and showing your working.

Example   154 g   ⇒ $\begin{array}{r} 273\ g \\ +\ 154\ g \\ \hline 427\ g \end{array}$
              273g

1   125 kg   **4**   522 tonnes   **7**   256 mg
    418 kg   298 tonnes   308 mg

2   317 kg   **5**   133 tonnes   **8**   845 kg
    290 kg   226 tonnes   253 kg

3   455 g   **6**   499 g   **9**   172 tonnes
    368 g   206 g   345 tonnes

F By setting out the weights in columns and showing your working, find out how much heavier one weight is than the other in each of the boxes in **E**.

G Look at this diagram. Write down how far it is from:
Example   cinema ➜ shops ➜ burger bar   ⇒   107 m + 96 m = 203 m

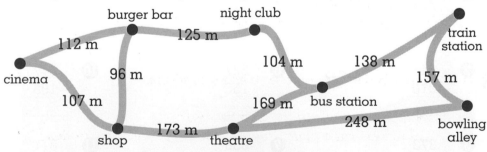

1   train station ➜ bus station ➜ night club
2   bowling alley ➜ theatre ➜ bus station
3   burger bar ➜ shops ➜ theatre
4   bus station ➜ night club ➜ burger bar
5   train station ➜ bowling alley ➜ theatre
6   train station ➜ bowling alley ➜ train station

H These are the crowd figures for two clubs over a series of Saturdays.

date	Fortnum Flyers	Soulsford City
2 February	1244	3104
9 February	1812	2399
16 February	2667	2711
23 February	2046	3262
1 March	1503	2430
8 March	2838	2309

Work out:

Example the total attendance on 2 February ⇒

$$\begin{array}{r} 1244 \\ + 3104 \\ \hline 4348 \end{array}$$ people

❶ the difference in the two attendances on 23 February
❷ the sum of the attendances at Soulsford City on 23 February and 1 March
❸ the difference in the two attendances on 2 February
❹ take away the attendance at Soulsford City on 8 March from that of Fortnum Flyers on the same day
❺ add the two attendances for Soulsford City over the dates 1 March and 8 March
❻ the difference in the attendances on 9 February

I Using the table in **H** , answer these questions.

❶ How many days were there in February?
❷ What is the name given to a year with that number of days in February?

Multiplication and Division

J Copy and complete the multiplication table.

	1	2	3	4	5	6	7	8	9	10
1										
2		4								
3					15					
4										
5				20						
6										
7							49			
8								72		
9			27							
10						60				

K From the multiplication table find all the ways of getting an answer of:
Example $16 \Rightarrow 2 \times 8$, 4×4, 8×2

1 20
2 24
3 25
4 36
5 42

6 12
7 63
8 64
9 30

L Complete each multiplication and then use the same numbers in a division.
Example $3 \times \underline{6} = 18 \Rightarrow 18 \div 3 = 6$

1 ___ $\times 7 = 42$
2 $5 \times$ ___ $= 40$
3 ___ $\times 9 = 27$
4 $8 \times$ ___ $= 48$
5 ___ $\times 7 = 56$

6 $9 \times$ ___ $= 72$
7 ___ $\times$ ___ $= 9$
8 ___ $\times$ ___ $= 49$
9 ___ $\times$ ___ $= 81$

M These are some of the cash prizes to be won in a raffle.

1st prize £150
2nd prize £112
3rd prize £78
4th prize £36
5th prize £24

Share the winnings equally in the questions below.
Example a group of four people wins 2nd prize ⇒ £112 ÷ 4 = £28

1 a group of six people wins 3rd prize
2 a group of eight people wins 5th prize
3 a group of five people wins 1st prize
4 a group of nine people wins 4th prize

N These are the amounts of rain that fell over different numbers of days.
Copy and complete the table showing the rainfall each day.

	total rainfall (mm)	number of days	rainfall per day	
Example	68 mm	4	17 mm	68 ÷ 4 = 17
1	72 mm	6		
2		7	5 mm	
3	96 mm	8		
4	70 mm	5		
5	87 mm	3		
6		6	9 mm	
7	99 mm	9		
8	91 mm	7		
9	128 mm	8		

O Copy and complete each of these multiplications, showing your working.

Example

$$\begin{array}{r} 32 \\ \times\ 2 \\ \hline 64 \end{array}$$

1
$$\begin{array}{r} 24 \\ \times\ 2 \\ \hline \end{array}$$

5
$$\begin{array}{r} 26 \\ \times\ 2 \\ \hline \end{array}$$

9
$$\begin{array}{r} 21 \\ \times\ 7 \\ \hline \end{array}$$

2
$$\begin{array}{r} 31 \\ \times\ 3 \\ \hline \end{array}$$

6
$$\begin{array}{r} 38 \\ \times\ 2 \\ \hline \end{array}$$

10
$$\begin{array}{r} 34 \\ \times\ 4 \\ \hline \end{array}$$

3
$$\begin{array}{r} 22 \\ \times\ 4 \\ \hline \end{array}$$

7
$$\begin{array}{r} 27 \\ \times\ 3 \\ \hline \end{array}$$

11
$$\begin{array}{r} 56 \\ \times\ 3 \\ \hline \end{array}$$

4
$$\begin{array}{r} 11 \\ \times\ 5 \\ \hline \end{array}$$

8
$$\begin{array}{r} 41 \\ \times\ 3 \\ \hline \end{array}$$

P Complete these divisions by setting them out as shown.

Example $48 \div 4 \Rightarrow 4\overline{)48}$ with 12 above.

1 $84 \div 4$

6 $240 \div 8$

11 $184 \div 8$

16 $216 \div 8$

2 $88 \div 8$

7 $160 \div 4$

12 $200 \div 4$

17 $112 \div 4$

3 $44 \div 4$

8 $128 \div 4$

13 $360 \div 8$

18 $216 \div 4$

4 $120 \div 4$

9 $328 \div 8$

14 $92 \div 4$

19 $384 \div 8$

5 $168 \div 8$

10 $96 \div 8$

15 $64 \div 4$

20 $472 \div 8$

✓ **Checking your answers**   ? **Testing how much you know**

Number Crunching 4

This chapter is about deciding which number rule to use (+, −, × or ÷) to solve a problem. Calculators can be used throughout but working out should be shown as well.

Useful information

a signs

sum
add
total
altogether
$\left.\right\}$ = **+**

take away
difference
left over
more than
$\left.\right\}$ = **−**

times
multiply
lots of
$\left.\right\}$ = **×**

share
divide
split
$\left.\right\}$ = **÷**

b always check to see if your answer is sensible, by estimating with rounded numbers

2 Number Crunching 1
3 Number Crunching 2
13 Number Crunching 3

SUPPORT: S19, S20
EXTENSION: E1, E2, E10

Deciding When to Use +, −, × and ÷

A Decide if these questions need + or − and then use a calculator to work out the answers.

Example A man has £200 and spends £46. How much is left?
⇒ £200 − £46 = £154

① There are 262 fish in one lake, and 179 fish in another lake. How many fish are there altogether?

② A car travels 453 km and then a further 209 km. How far does it travel altogether?

③ Two people together weigh 173 kg. If one of them weighs 84 kg, how much does the other weigh?

④ One road is 270 km long and another is 84 km. How much longer is the first road?

⑤ A woman has two bank accounts, one with £125 and the other with £97. How much does she have altogether?

⑥ What is the difference in weight between a horse weighing 282 kg and another horse weighing 307 kg?

⑦ A man saves £1000 and then spends £693 on a holiday. How much does he have left?

B Decide if these questions need × or ÷ and then use a calculator to work out the answers.

Example A holiday costs £256 each. How much is it for a family of 4? ⇒ £256 × 4 = £1024

① A train carries 1244 people spread evenly over 4 carriages. How many people are there in each carriage?

② A prize of £12 360 is shared equally among 5 people. How much do they each get?

❸ The 5 men in a basketball team each weigh 85 kg. How much does the team weigh altogether?

❹ Each footballer needs 12 studs for his boots. How many studs are needed for a team of 11 players?

❺ A hotel has 56 rooms and each room sleeps 6 people. How many people can the hotel sleep?

❻ A cinema has 8 screens and has 1440 people spread equally between each screen. How many people are watching each screen?

❼ A bookshop has 21 750 books spread out evenly over 25 shelves. How many books fit on each shelf?

Working Out Problems With +, − × and ÷

C The table shows the produce of a farm on one day.

produce	amount
potatoes	420 kg
sweetcorn	236 cobs
cauliflowers	87
carrots	325 kg
peas	78 kg
swedes	192 kg

Use a calculator to work out the following.

Example　If the potatoes are packed in 12-kg bags, how many bags are needed? $\Rightarrow$ 420 kg ÷ 12 = 35 bags

❶ How many sweetcorn cobs would be produced in 4 days?
❷ If the peas are put evenly into 26 bags, find the weight (in kg) in each bag.
❸ How many cauliflowers would be produced in one week?
❹ Find the total weight of potatoes and carrots produced in one day.
❺ Find the difference in weight between the swedes and peas produced in one day.
❻ Find the weight of potatoes produced in 2 weeks.

D These are the scores of players in a darts match. To win a score of 501 is needed.

name	score
Andy	87
Chris	204
Anthea	126
Isobel	117
Frankie	285

Work out the answers to these questions.

Example How much more has Frankie scored than Andy?

$$\Rightarrow 285 - 87 = 198 \text{ more}$$

1. Anthea has taken 6 darts to reach her score. If each dart scored the same number, what was the score with each dart?
2. How many more does Chris need to win?
3. What is the difference between Frankie's score and Isobel's?
4. What is the total of Chris and Andy's scores?
5. How much more does Anthea need to win?
6. Andy has thrown 6 darts. If the first 5 were all 15, then what was the score for the sixth dart?
7. How many more points does Andy need to win than Isobel?

E Copy and complete this table of wages earned in a week.

	name	hours worked	pay per hour	wages
Example	Tom	35	£4.20	35 × 4.20 = £147.00
1	David	42	£7.60	
2	Julian	36	£8.20	
3	James		£4.00	= £160.00
4	Tina		£12.10	= £471.90
5	Robert		£2.97	= £109.89
6	Lisa	41		= £332.10
7	Jackie	18		= £105.30

F These are the prices for Sunday lunch in a country pub.

Sunday lunch   £4.25
Coffee   £0.70
House wine   £5.95

Work out each bill.
Example Sunday lunch × 4 ⇒ £4.25 × 4 = £17.00

1 Sunday lunch × 2
    Coffee × 2

4 Sunday lunch × 7
    Coffee × 3
    House wine × 2

2 Sunday lunch × 3
    House wine × 2

5 Sunday lunch × 12
    Coffee × 8
    House wine × 4

3 Sunday lunch × 6
    Coffee × 4
    House wine × 1

G Each of these motorists was caught speeding. If the fine is £4 for each mile per hour (mph) over the speed limit, complete the table.

	name	speed	speed limit	fine
Example	Tim	37 mph	30 mph	7 × £4 = £28
1	Andrea	84 mph	60 mph	
2	Lucy	105 mph	70 mph	
3	Elliott		70 mph	○ × 4 = £ 60
4	Annette		60 mph	○ × 4 = £180
5	Tony		40 mph	○ × 4 = £108
6	Naveed	88 mph	60 mph	28 × 4 = £112
7	Megan	57 mph		○ × 4 = £ 68

105

H Copy and complete the table to show prices for rented accommodation for a week.

	accommodation	price	number sharing	price each
Example	Caravan	£348	6	£348 ÷ 6 = £58
❶	Cottage	£285	5	
❷	Bedsit		4	= £37
❸	Flat	£225		= £45
❹	Bungalow		5	= £81
❺	Hotel	£644	4	
❻	Bed & Breakfast	£432		= £72
❼	Hostel		10	= £45

Decimals 1

This chapter is about reading and marking onto decimal scales. It looks at numbers with one or two decimal places.

Useful information

a each whole number can be shared into ten or as many as a hundred pieces to show a more accurate measure. This is called a **decimal number**. We use a **decimal point** to keep the whole numbers separate from tenths and hundredths

so 1 + 7 tenths = 1.7
      1 + 27 hundredths = 1.27
      1 + 2 tenths + 7 hundredths = 1.27

b when you put decimal numbers in order, tenths are bigger than hundredths

so 1.3 is bigger than 1.23 because there are more tenths in 1.3 than in 1.23

Ch 1 Place Value 1

Ch 23 Decimals 2
WORKSHEET: W3

Reading Decimal Scales

A Write down the number that each arrow marks.

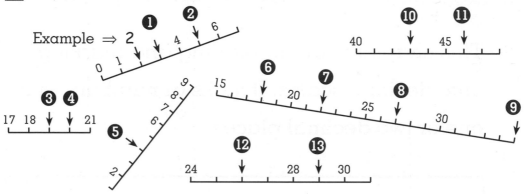

B Write down the number that each arrow marks.

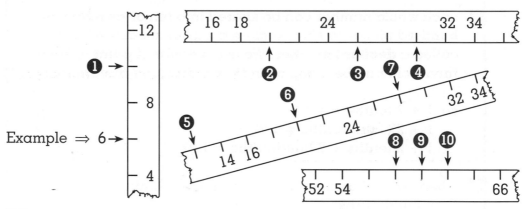

C Write down the number that each arrow marks.

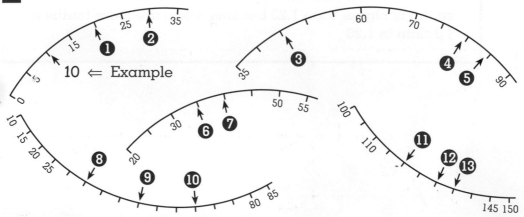

D Write down the number that each arrow marks.

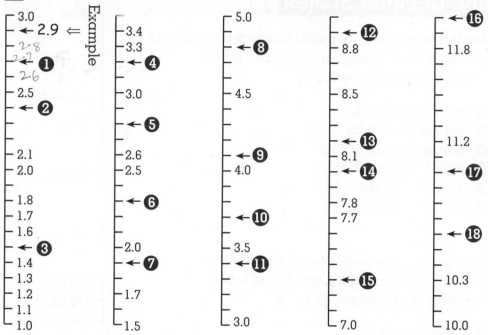

E These scales are marked differently. Write down the number that each arrow marks.

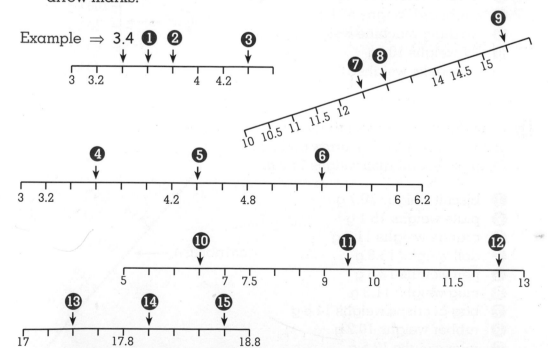

Using Decimal Scales

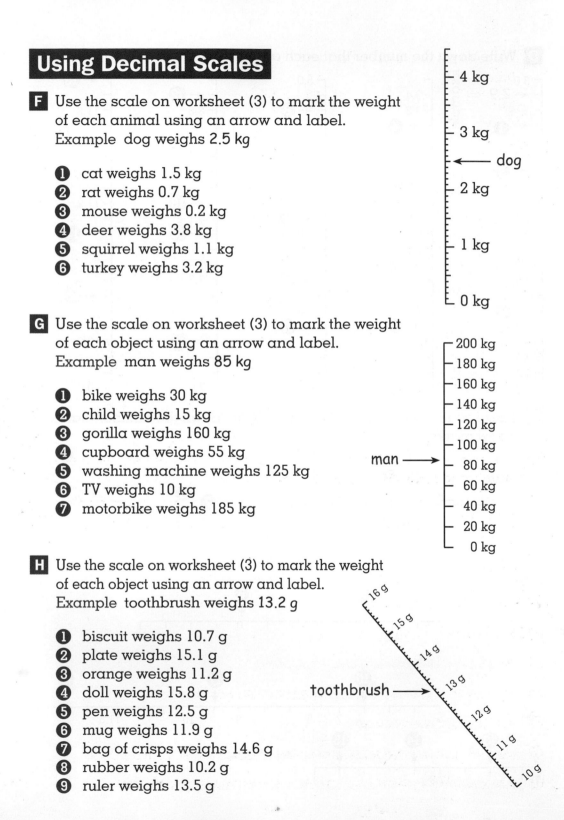

F Use the scale on worksheet (3) to mark the weight
of each animal using an arrow and label.
Example dog weighs 2.5 kg

1 cat weighs 1.5 kg
2 rat weighs 0.7 kg
3 mouse weighs 0.2 kg
4 deer weighs 3.8 kg
5 squirrel weighs 1.1 kg
6 turkey weighs 3.2 kg

G Use the scale on worksheet (3) to mark the weight
of each object using an arrow and label.
Example man weighs 85 kg

1 bike weighs 30 kg
2 child weighs 15 kg
3 gorilla weighs 160 kg
4 cupboard weighs 55 kg
5 washing machine weighs 125 kg
6 TV weighs 10 kg
7 motorbike weighs 185 kg

H Use the scale on worksheet (3) to mark the weight
of each object using an arrow and label.
Example toothbrush weighs 13.2 g

1 biscuit weighs 10.7 g
2 plate weighs 15.1 g
3 orange weighs 11.2 g
4 doll weighs 15.8 g
5 pen weighs 12.5 g
6 mug weighs 11.9 g
7 bag of crisps weighs 14.6 g
8 rubber weighs 10.2 g
9 ruler weighs 13.5 g

I Trace these decimal scales, and complete the numbers on each of them.

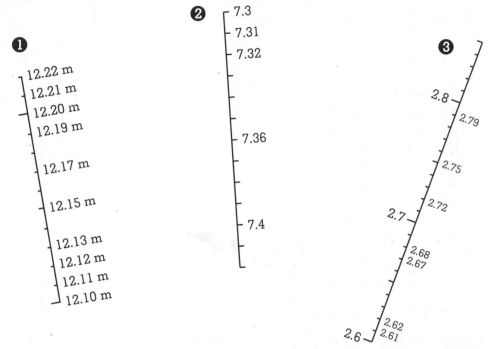

J The end of each object and scale is shown. The other end is at the start of the scale. How long is each object?

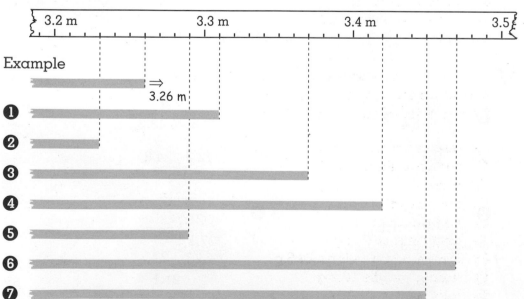

Example

⇒ 3.26 m

1

2

3

4

5

6

7

K The end of each pole and scale is shown. The other end is at the start of the scale. How long is each pole?

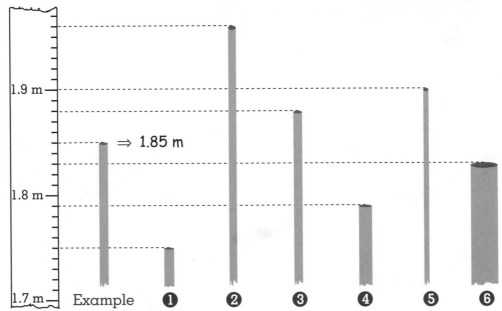

⇒ 1.85 m

1.9 m

1.8 m

1.7 m   Example   ❶   ❷   ❸   ❹   ❺   ❻

Ordering Decimal Numbers

L List each group of numbers in order, smallest first.

Example   3.4   4.7   1.5   6.9   5.3   ⇒ 1.5, 3.4, 4.7, 5.3, 6.9

❶   2.7   5.4   3.6   6.3   4.5

❷   1.9   1.1   9.9   9.1   1.5   5.1

❸   32.4   23.4   43.2   42.3   24.3

❹   21.7   22.7   27.1   27.7   27.2   21.1

M List each group of numbers in order, smallest first.

Example

3.58
3.61
3.45
3.16
3.27

⇒ 3.16, 3.27, 3.45, 3.58, 3.61

❶
5.18   5.33
5.29   5.22
5.15
5.23

❸
3.55   5.55
3.35
5.35   5.33
5.53

❷
6.29   6.62
6.69   6.96
6.92
6.66

❹
8.32
2.22   8.33
8.23
2.82   8.22

N List these numbers in order, largest first.

2.7   7.7
7.2   2.72
7.22   2.77   7.72   7.27
2.2   7.77
        2.22   2.27

Checking your answers   **Testing how much you know**

Money

This chapter is about using money and working out bills up to £10.

Useful information

a 100p = £1.00

so   130p = £1.30
      229p = £2.29
       50p = £0.50
        7p = £0.07

b when you add or subtract money you must keep the decimal points under each other

e.g.

c to add or take away with money you should have all the amounts in the same units (all in £s only, or all in £s and pence, or all in pence only)

Ch 2 Number Crunching
Ch 3 Number Crunching
Ch 13 Number Crunching
Ch 14 Number Crunching
Ch 15 Decimals 1

Ch 23 Decimals 2

Working with Pounds and Pence

A Using a variety of coins from the panel, find ten different ways to make exactly £1.

Example 50p + 20p + 20p + 5p + 5p = £1

50p
10p   2p
20p
5p   1p

B Find the number of 10 pence pieces in each amount of money.

Example 20p ⇒ two 10 pence pieces

1 50p
2 10p
3 60p
4 70p
5 40p

6 30p
7 90p
8 80p
9 £1.00
10 £1.10

C Find the number of 5 pence pieces in each amount of money.

Example 20p ⇒ four 5 pence pieces

1 10p
2 15p
3 30p
4 25p
5 40p

6 60p
7 55p
8 80p
9 75p
10 95p

D Find the number of 2 pence pieces in each amount of money.

Example 20p ⇒ ten 2 pence pieces

1 6p
2 12p
3 18p
4 10p
5 24p

6 30p
7 28p
8 50p
9 36p
10 42p

E Work out the total value in pence.
Example 20p + 10p + 10p = 40p

1 20p + 20p + 10p =
2 50p + 20p + 10p =
3 20p + 10p +5p =
4 50p + 5p + 5p =
5 20p + 5p + 2p =

6 50p + 2p +1p =
7 20p + 20p +2p +1p =
8 50p + 5p + 2p + 2p =
9 50p + 20p + 10p + 5p + 2p + 1p =
10 50p + 5p +5p +2p +2p +2p =

F Work out the total value in £s.
Example £1 + 50p +10p = 160p = £1.60

1 £1 + 20p + 20p
2 £1 + 10p + 5p
3 £1 + 20p + 10p + 5p
4 £1 + 10p + 5p + 5p
5 £1 + £1 + 50p

6 £1 + £1 + 20p + 10p
7 £1 + £1 + £1 + 5p + 5p
8 £1 + £1 + 20p + 10p + 2p
9 £1 + 5p + 2p + 2p + 1p
10 £1 + £1 + 5p + 1p

G Change each of these into £s.
Example 200p = £2.00

1 350p
2 227p
3 440p
4 352p
5 70p

6 105p
7 207p
8 409p
9 7p
10 9p

H Change each of these into pence.
Example £3.00 = 300p

1 £2.60
2 £1.44
3 £3.21
4 £5.52
5 £0.80

6 £3.05
7 £1.08
8 £0.41
9 £0.02
10 £0.04

I Put the amounts of money in each bag in order, smallest first.

Example  ⇒ £0.50, 70p, £1.20, 160p

①

②

③

J Change these calculator numbers into money (p).
Example 0.3 ⇒ 30p

① 0.27   **⑥** 0.6
② 0.32   **⑦** 0.2
③ 0.58   **⑧** 0.9
④ 0.04   **⑨** 0.01
⑤ 0.05   **⑩** 0.7

K Change these calculator numbers into money (£).
Example 1.4 ⇒ £1.40

① 1.37   **⑥** 5.1
② 1.42   **⑦** 3.9
③ 2.71   **⑧** 2.03
④ 3.2   **⑨** 1.01
⑤ 1.8   **⑩** 5.08

Working Out the Total

L Find the total in each bag in pounds (£).

Example

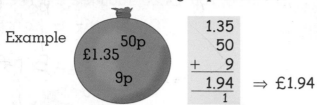

50p
£1.35
9p

```
  1.35
  50
+  9
────
  1.94      ⇒ £1.94
  1
```

1
70p
27p
£1.01

3
£2
8p
60p

5
£3.25
£2   40p
9p

2
32p
5p   £1.20

4
£1
12p   42p
£2.35

M Work out the total value of these bills by setting them out in columns.

Example

42p
21p
13p

```
  42
  21
+ 13
────
  76      ⇒ 76p
```

1
12p
15p
17p

3
12p
12p
12p
12p

5
23p
30p
17p
11p

2
12p
41p
33p

4
17p
11p
31p

N Work out each bill by setting the sums out in columns.

Example hat + tie

$$
\begin{array}{r}
3.90 \\
2.50 \\
\hline
6.40
\end{array} \Rightarrow £6.40
$$

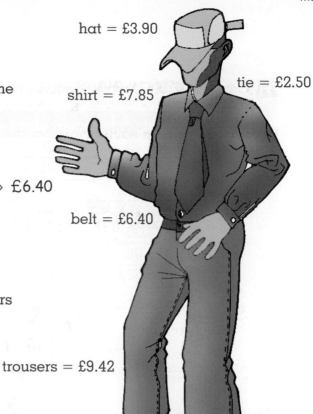

hat = £3.90

tie = £2.50

shirt = £7.85

belt = £6.40

trousers = £9.42

❶ trousers + belt
❷ shirt + tie
❸ shirt + belt + tie
❹ hat + shirt + belt + trousers
❺ tie + belt + trousers

Working Out the Change

O Copy the table and work out the change needed.

	cost	amount given	change needed
Example	32p	£1	100p – 32p = 68p
❶	20p	£1	
❷	50p	£1	
❸	70p	£1	
❹	65p	£1	
❺	15p	£1	
❻	27p	£1	
❼	43p	£1	
❽	6p	£1	
❾	4p	£1	
❿	89p	£1	

P Copy the table and work out the change needed.

	cost	amount given	change needed
Example	£2.40	£5	500p – 240p = £2.60
1	£2	£5	
2	£1.50	£5	
3	£4.70	£5	
4	£3.20	£5	
5	£1.06	£5	
6	58p	£5	
7	81p	£5	
8	£1.15	£5	
9	£4.65	£5	
10	£3.99	£5	

Q Copy the table and work out the change needed.

	cost	amount given	change needed
Example	£5.70	£10	1000p – 570p = £4.30
1	£6	£10	
2	£3.80	£10	
3	£7.10	£10	
4	£9.30	£10	
5	70p	£10	
6	45p	£10	
7	£2.55	£10	
8	£5.05	£10	
9	£7.17	£10	
10	£3.99	£10	

Money Problems

R In a sponsored swim people sponsored Dave for each length of the pool. Work out the total money that each sponsor must pay.

	sponsor	amount per length	total	paid
Name: Dave **Distance: 12 lengths**				
Example	Mum	50p	50p × 12 = 600p = £6.00	✔
❶	Dad	40p		
❷	Gran	20p		✔
❸	Mr Thomas	10p		✔
❹	Miss Jones	12p		
❺	Jimmy	5p		✔
❻	Aunt Anne	9p		
❼	Mrs Walker	7p		
❽	Mr Morgan	15p		✔
❾	Andrew J.	8p		✔

❿ How much will Dave get for each length?
⓫ How many people have paid him so far?
⓬ How much money has he collected?

S On a sponsored walk Anne raised money for charity. Work out the total money that each sponsor must pay.

	sponsor	amount per km	total	paid
15 km walk for charity **Name: Anne**				
Example	Ted	10p	10p × 15 = 150p = £1.50	✔
❶	Mum	25p		✔
❷	Grandad	15p		✔
❸	Uncle Jim	9p		
❹	Debbie	5p		✔
❺	Joanna	7p		
❻	Kelly	2p		✔
❼	Sian	8p		

T Work out the total cost of each of these bills on a calculator.

1
Dog food 32p
Dog food 32p
Dog food 32p
Dog food 32p

2
Toothbrush £1.55
Toothbrush £1.55
Soap   45p
Soap   45p
Soap   45p
Toothpaste £1.89

U Work out the total cost for each item, and the total bill using a calculator.

	item	price	amount	total price
Mick's Discount Shop				
Example	can of beans	17p	10	17p × 10 = 170p = £1.70
1	toilet rolls	47p	4	
2	packet soups	73p	6	
3	box of tissues	£1.12	5	
4	bin-bags	89p	12	
5	biscuits	40p	22	
6	apples	13p	50	
7			Total	

V You have lots of each of the stamps in the panel. Find the fewest stamps you can use for each of these packages.

Example   17p = 12p + 5p

1p
5p   12p
2p £1
25p

1   79p

4   £2.62

2   £1.22

5   £1.98

3   £3.38

✓ **Checking your answers**   **Testing how much you know**

Negative Numbers

This chapter is about using numbers below 0 such as in very cold temperatures, or overdrafts at a bank.

Useful information

a

6
5
4   warmer   go up the scale
3   when adding
2
1
0   zero (freezing point of water)
− 1
− 2
− 3   colder   go down the scale
− 4   when subtracting
− 5
− 6

b to work out questions with negative numbers, always draw a scale

e.g.
to work out 4 − 7, start at 4 and go down 7 spaces to find the answer, − 3
to work out − 3 + 2, start at − 3 and go up 2 spaces to find the answer, − 1

Ch 5 Patterns
Ch 15 Decimals 1

EXTENSION: E3

Temperatures

A Copy and complete each of the temperature scales.

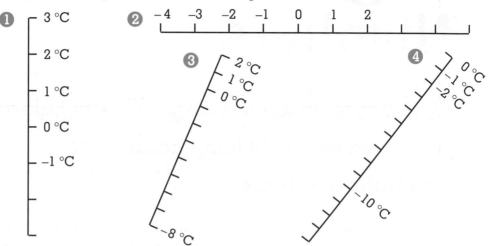

B What temperature do each of these thermometers show?

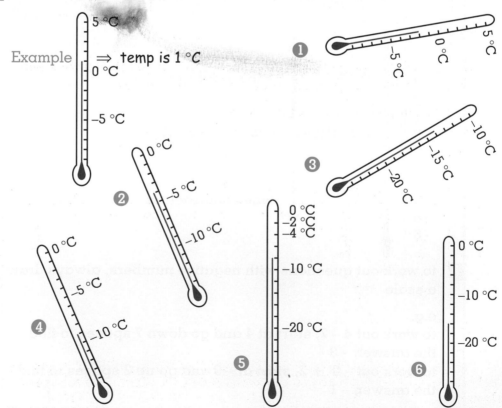

C This bar chart shows the temperature in London at different times of a day. Copy and complete the table below.

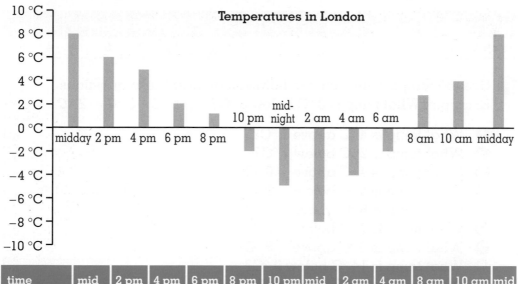

time	mid day	2 pm	4 pm	6 pm	8 pm	10 pm	mid night	2 am	4 am	8 am	10 am	mid day
Temp. (°C)	8 °C			2 °C								

D This bar chart shows the average monthly temperatures over one year in Norway. Copy and complete the table below.

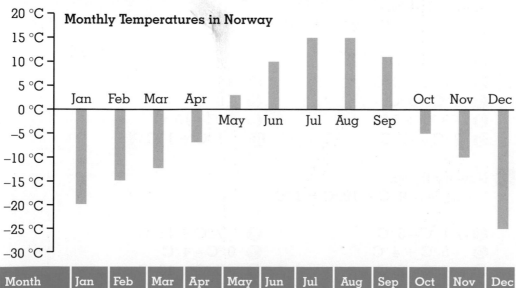

Month	Jan	Feb	Mar	Apr	May	Jun	Jul	Aug	Sep	Oct	Nov	Dec
Temp (°C)					2.5°C					− 5°C		

E Draw a bar chart like those in **C** and **D** using the table below of night time temperatures in Glasgow.

Time	Mon	Tues	Wed	Thurs	Fri	Sat	Sun	Mon	Tues	Wed	Thurs	Fri	Sat	Sun
Temp °C	4	-2	-5	4	1	7	-2	-8	-10	-3	-6	1	4	5

F Use the temperature scale to help you answer these questions.
Example What temp is 3 °C below 5 °C? $\Rightarrow$ 5 °C – 3 °C = 2 °C

1. What temp is 4 °C above 1 °C?
2. What temp is 2 °C below 1 °C?
3. What temp is 4 °C above – 6 °C?
4. What temp is 5 °C below – 2 °C?
5. What temp is 6 °C above – 3 °C?
6. What temp is 7 °C below – 1 °C
7. What temp is 9 °C above – 9 °C?
8. What temp is 14 °C below 9 °C?
9. What temp is 17 °C above – 8 °C?

Temperature in °C

10, 9, 8, 7, 6, 5, 4, 3, 2, 1, 0, –1, –2, –3, –4, –5, –6, –7, –8, –9, –10

Negative Number Calculations

G Draw a scale from 10 to – 10 like the one in **F** to help you answer these questions.
Example – 1 °C + 2 °C = 1 °C

1. 4 °C – 7 °C
2. – 2 °C + 3 °C
3. 5 °C – 9 °C
4. – 3 °C + 5 °C
5. 7 °C – 11 °C
6. – 7 °C + 2 °C
7. 3 °C – 9 °C
8. – 8 °C + 4 °C
9. 1 °C – 10 °C
10. – 1 °C + 1 °C

H Now try these.
Example – 9 °C + 10 °C = 1 °C

1. – 1 °C – 3 °C
2. – 5 °C + 4 °C
3. – 4 °C – 2 °C
4. – 8 °C + 8 °C
5. – 3 °C – 7 °C
6. – 7 °C + 11 °C
7. 0 °C – 4 °C
8. – 9 °C + 13 °C
9. – 5 °C – 5 °C
10. – 10 °C + 11 °C

I Copy this scale to help you answer these by counting in tens.

Example $50 - 30 = 20$

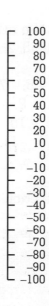

① $30 - 50$
② $20 - 60$
③ $10 - 30$
④ $-10 - 20$
⑤ $-20 + 30$
⑥ $-10 + 20$
⑦ $-40 + 80$
⑧ $-50 + 30$
⑨ $-90 + 40$

J Fill in the missing part of each question.

Example $2 - \underline{3} = -1$

① $-7 + \underline{} = -6$
② $-4 + \underline{} = 0$
③ $-1 - \underline{} = -5$
④ $\underline{} + 2 = 0$
⑤ $\underline{} - 7 = -3$

⑥ $3 - \underline{} = -5$
⑦ $-5 + \underline{} = 1$
⑧ $-7 + \underline{} = 6$
⑨ $\underline{} - 2 = -8$

Negative Number Patterns

K Fill in the next two numbers in each of these patterns.

Example $8, 6, 4, 2, 0, -2, \underline{-4}, \underline{-6}$ Rule $\Rightarrow -2$

① $9, 6, 3, 0, -3, \underline{}, \underline{}$ Rule $\Rightarrow -3$
② $-8, -5, -2, \underline{}, \underline{}$ Rule $\Rightarrow +3$
③ $-4, -8, -12, -16, \underline{}, \underline{}$ Rule $\Rightarrow -4$
④ $9, 4, -1, \underline{}, \underline{}$ Rule $\Rightarrow -5$
⑤ $-18, -15, -12, \underline{}, \underline{}$ Rule $\Rightarrow +3$
⑥ $15, 9, 3, -3, \underline{}, \underline{}$ Rule $\Rightarrow -6$

L What is the rule that makes each of these patterns work?

Example $5, 2, -1, -4, -7, -10$ Rule $\Rightarrow -3$

1 $-5, -6, -7, -8, -9$ Rule $\Rightarrow$
2 $-11, -9, -7, -5, -3$ Rule $\Rightarrow$
3 $-15, -10, -5, 0, 5$ Rule $\Rightarrow$
4 $3, -4, -11, -18, -25$ Rule $\Rightarrow$

M Arrange each of these lists of temperatures in order, coldest first.

1

2

Checking your answers   **Testing how much you know**

Number Machines

This chapter is about using number machines to solve problems. The machine shows the operation on a number that is put in. The number that comes out is also shown.

2 Number Crunching 1
3 Number Crunching 2
3 Number Crunching 3

Ch 30 Finding Rules
1 Backwards Calculations
Ch 32 Formulas

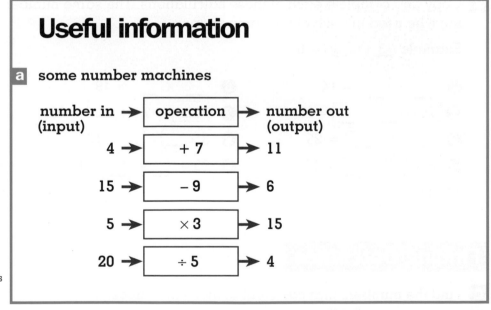

Useful information

a   some number machines

number in (input) → | operation | → number out (output)

$4 \rightarrow$ | $+ 7$ | $\rightarrow 11$

$15 \rightarrow$ | $- 9$ | $\rightarrow 6$

$5 \rightarrow$ | $\times 3$ | $\rightarrow 15$

$20 \rightarrow$ | $\div 5$ | $\rightarrow 4$

Completing Calculations

A Copy and complete each of these calculations.

Example $4 + \langle \underline{7} \rangle = 11$

1. $\bigcirc + 8 = 13$
2. $15 - \bigcirc = 4$
3. $8 + \boxed{} = 19$
4. $23 - \boxed{} = 8$
5. $3 \times \langle \rangle = 15$

6. $\pentagon + 17 = 26$
7. $24 \div \triangle = 4$
8. $\boxed{} - 12 = 19$
9. $\bigcirc \times 3 = 21$

B Copy and complete each of these calculations. The same number must be used in each of the same shapes.

Example $\bigcirc 3 + \bigcirc 3 = 6$

1. $\hexagon + \hexagon = 14$
2. $20 - \boxed{} - \boxed{} = 16$
3. $\boxed{} \times \boxed{} = 25$
4. $3 + \bigcirc + \bigcirc = 15$
5. $45 - \pentagon - \pentagon = 23$

6. $\bigcirc \times \bigcirc = 49$
7. $\boxed{} + 7 + \boxed{} = 23$
8. $3 \times \bigcirc \times \bigcirc = 12$
9. $25 \div \triangle \div \triangle = 1$

Finding Outcomes

C Find the numbers that come out of these machines.

Example $3 \rightarrow \boxed{+ 4} \rightarrow 7$

1. $7 \rightarrow \boxed{+6} \rightarrow$
2. $15 \rightarrow \boxed{- 8} \rightarrow$
3. $3 \rightarrow \boxed{\times 3} \rightarrow$
4. $12 \rightarrow \boxed{\div 2} \rightarrow$
5. $10 \rightarrow \boxed{+11} \rightarrow$

6. $15 \rightarrow \boxed{\div 3} \rightarrow$
7. $20 \rightarrow \boxed{\times 1} \rightarrow$
8. $10 \rightarrow \boxed{\div 5} \rightarrow$
9. $25 \rightarrow \boxed{- 13} \rightarrow$

D Find the number that comes out when the given numbers are put into the machine.

Example
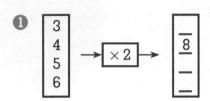

①

②
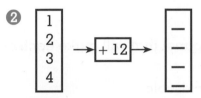

③
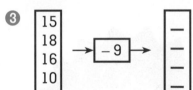

④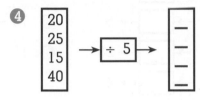

⑤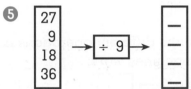

Finding Operations 1

E From the panel, find the operation which fits in the machine to make the machine work.

Example 2 → + 2 → 4

① 4 → ☐ → 7

② 8 → ☐ → 5

③ 5 → ☐ → 10

④ 7 → ☐ → 11

⑤ 1 → ☐ → 8

⑥ 10 → ☐ → 3

⑦ 6 → ☐ → 1

⑧ 15 → ☐ → 4

⑨ 3 → ☐ → 15

− 11
+ 12   + 3
− 3   + 2
− 5   − 7
+ 5
+ 4   + 7

F This time the machines use operations with × and ÷. The operations needed are in the panel. Choose the right operation.

Example   2 → ×2 → 4

1   2 → ☐ → 6   **6**   9 → ☐ → 3

2   3 → ☐ → 6   **7**   1 → ☐ → 4

3   10 → ☐ → 5   **8**   10 → ☐ → 2

4   5 → ☐ → 25   **9**   10 → ☐ → 100

5   16 → ☐ → 4

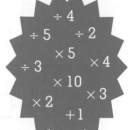

÷4   ÷5   ÷2   ×5   ÷3   ×4   ×10   ×3   ×2   +1

G Find *all* the different operations in the panel that will make each of these machines work.

Example   2 → ☐ → 4 ⇒ × 2, +2 or double

1   3 → ☐ → 6

2   2 → ☐ → 1

3   10 → ☐ → 5

4   3 → ☐ → 12

5   8 → ☐ → 2

6   20 → ☐ → 2

7   3 → ☐ → 15

+2   ÷2   ×5   −5   halve   +9   quarter   −18   −6   +3   ÷4   ÷10   double   ×2   ×4   −1   +12

Multiple Machines

H Find what comes out of these double machines taking two steps.

Example 3 → | +4 | →⁷ | × 2 | → 14

❶ 4 → | − 1 | → | × 3 | →

❷ 8 → | ÷ 2 | → | + 3 | →

❸ 6 → | +3 | → | ÷ 3 | →

❹ 5 → | − 1 | → | ÷ 2 | →

❺ 4 → | × 2 | → | × 3 | →

❻ 14 → | ÷ 7 | → | − 3 | →

❼ 10 → | ÷ 2 | → | × 2 | →

❽ 20 → | ÷ 2 | → | ÷ 5 | →

❾ 6 → | × 5 | → | × 2 | →

I Find the number that comes out when the given numbers are put into the machines.

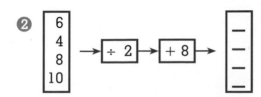

❶ | 3 4 5 6 | → | × 3 | →⁹ | − 7 | → | 2 — — — |

❷ | 6 4 8 10 | → | ÷ 2 | → | + 8 | → | — — — — |

J Find the numbers that come out of these longer machines when the given numbers are put in.

❶
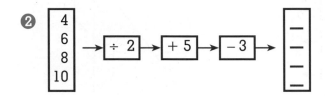
$$\begin{array}{|c|}1\\2\\3\\4\end{array} \rightarrow \boxed{\times 2} \rightarrow \boxed{-2} \rightarrow \boxed{+3} \rightarrow \begin{array}{|c|}\underline{3}\\\underline{}\\\underline{}\\\underline{}\end{array}$$

with small labels: 2 above ×2→−2, 0 above −2→+3

❷
$$\begin{array}{|c|}4\\6\\8\\10\end{array} \rightarrow \boxed{\div 2} \rightarrow \boxed{+5} \rightarrow \boxed{-3} \rightarrow \begin{array}{|c|}\underline{}\\\underline{}\\\underline{}\\\underline{}\end{array}$$

❸
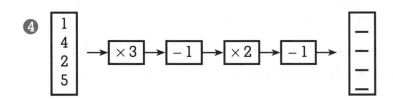
$$\begin{array}{|c|}9\\3\\12\\6\end{array} \rightarrow \boxed{\div 3} \rightarrow \boxed{+1} \rightarrow \boxed{\times 2} \rightarrow \boxed{-4} \rightarrow \begin{array}{|c|}\underline{}\\\underline{}\\\underline{}\\\underline{}\end{array}$$

❹
$$\begin{array}{|c|}1\\4\\2\\5\end{array} \rightarrow \boxed{\times 3} \rightarrow \boxed{-1} \rightarrow \boxed{\times 2} \rightarrow \boxed{-1} \rightarrow \begin{array}{|c|}\underline{}\\\underline{}\\\underline{}\\\underline{}\end{array}$$

❺
$$\begin{array}{|c|}10\\15\\5\\25\end{array} \rightarrow \boxed{\div 5} \rightarrow \boxed{\times 2} \rightarrow \boxed{+1} \rightarrow \boxed{\times 2} \rightarrow \begin{array}{|c|}\underline{}\\\underline{}\\\underline{}\\\underline{}\end{array}$$

Finding Operations 2

K Look at the panel to find the operation that makes the machine work.

Example

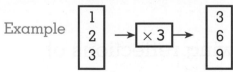

```
1          3
2  → ×3 → 6
3          9
```

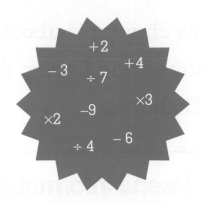

```
+2
−3      +4
    ÷7
        ×3
    −9
×2
        −6
  ÷4
```

1
```
4          8
7  → □ → 11
11         15
```

2
```
4          1
5  → □ → 2
6          3
```

3
```
12         3
16 → □ → 4
20         5
```

4
```
7          1
28 → □ → 4
14         2
21         3
```

L Complete the operation to make the machine work. Use the operations in the panel to help.

1
```
1                   3
2  → ×2 → □ → 5
3                   7
```

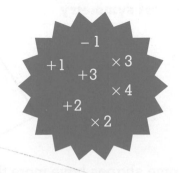

```
    −1
+1      ×3
    +3
        ×4
  +2
    ×2
```

2
```
4                   7
3  → □ → −1 → 5
2                   3
```

3
```
4                   15
5  → □ → +3 → 18
6                   21
```

 Checking your answers **Testing how much you know**

Symmetry 1

This chapter is about drawing reflections of shapes and finding the lines of symmetry of 2-D shapes.

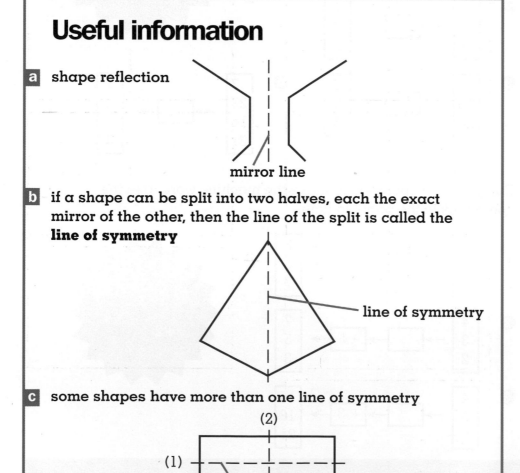

Useful information

a shape reflection

mirror line

b if a shape can be split into two halves, each the exact mirror of the other, then the line of the split is called the **line of symmetry**

line of symmetry

c some shapes have more than one line of symmetry

(2)

(1)

2 lines of symmetry ((1) and (2))

Ch 20 Symmetry 2

WORKSHEET: W4, W
W6, W7, W8

Reflection in a Mirror

A Using worksheet (4) and a mirror, put the mirror on the dashed line and draw the reflection.

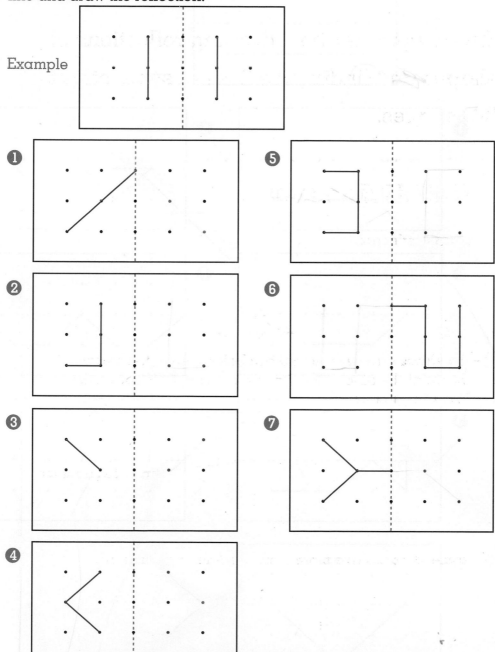

Example

1

2

3

4

5

6

7

B In these questions the mirror line goes across the page.
Use worksheet (5) to draw the reflection. You can use a mirror.

Example

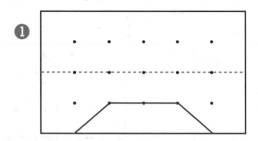

❶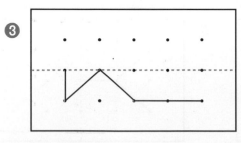

❺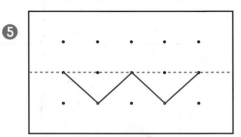

❷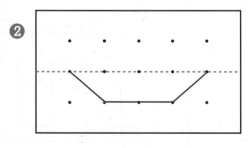

❻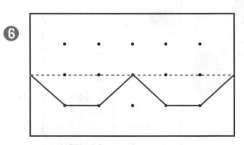

❸

❼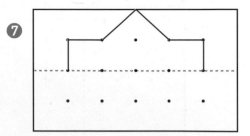

❹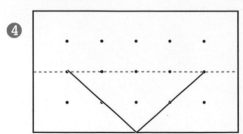

C Complete worksheet (6) where the mirror line is on a diagonal.

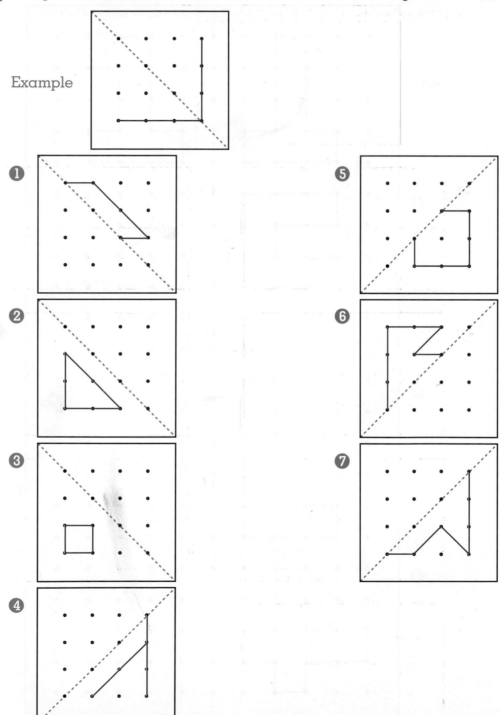

Example

D Use worksheet (7) to draw the reflection of these numbers.

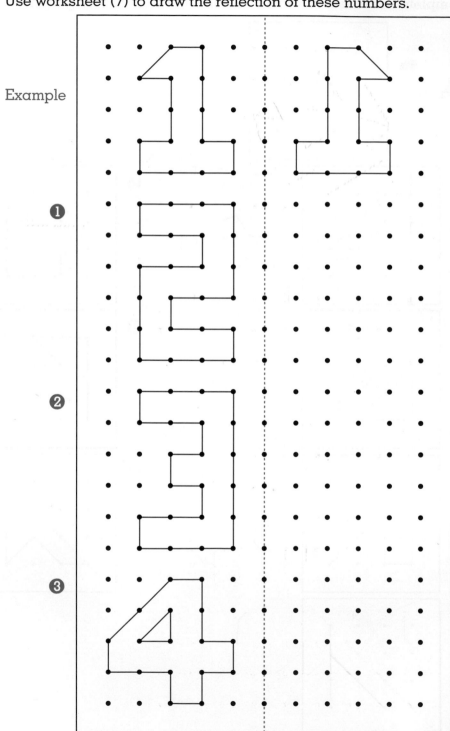

Example

❶

❷

❸

E Use worksheet (8) to draw the reflection of the shaded squares.

Example

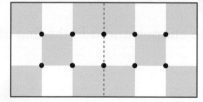

❶
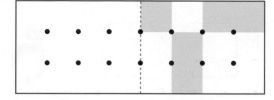

❷
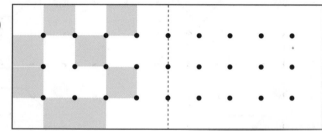

❸

❹
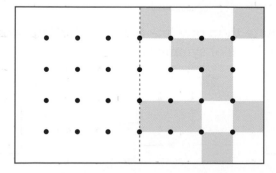

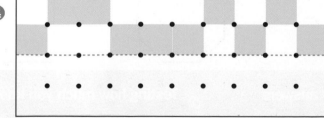

Lines of Symmetry

F Draw or trace each of these shapes and add the line of symmetry (a dotted line) to each one.

Example

① ④ ⑦

② ⑤ ⑧

③ ⑥ ⑨

G These shapes have more than one line of symmetry. Draw or trace each one and all their lines of symmetry.

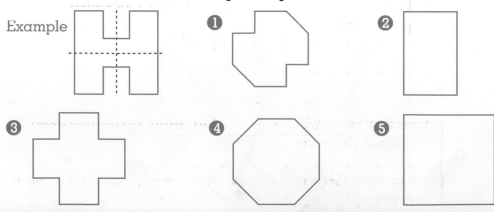

Example ① ②

③ ④ ⑤

✓ **Checking your answers**   ⊙ **Testing how much you know**

Symmetry 2

This chapter is about drawing reflections, rotations and translations of shapes. It also looks at congruent shapes.

Useful information

a **order of rotation** – the number of different positions in which a shape looks the same

    1   2   3   → order of rotation of 3

b **rotation** – turning a shape round a fixed point

$\frac{1}{2}$ turn → 180°   ⟳ → clockwise

$\frac{1}{4}$ turn → 90°   ↻ → anti-clockwise

c **translation** – sliding a shape left, right, up and/or down by a number of spaces

d **congruent shapes** – shapes which are exactly the same in every way

e **tessellations** – a collection of shapes that covers a large pattern, without overlapping or leaving any gaps

Ch 19 Symmetry 1

WORKSHEET: W9, W10, W11, W12, W13

Reflection

A Use worksheet (9) to draw the reflections of these shaded shapes.

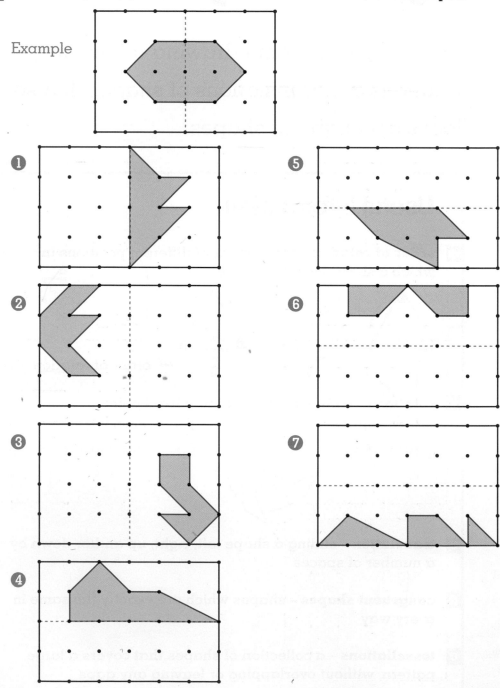

Example

1

2

3

4

5

6

7

B Use worksheet (10) to draw a reflection of the shaded shape. Then reflect this new shape and the given shape to fill all four sections.

Example

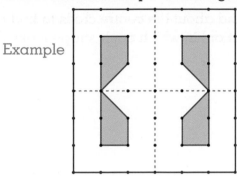

①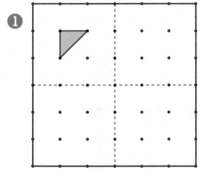

②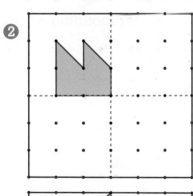

③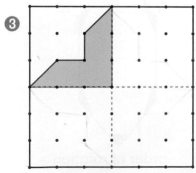

④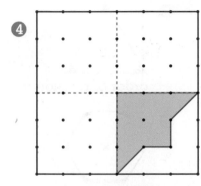

⑤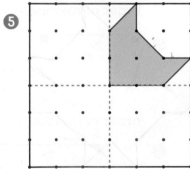

Rotation

C Trace each shape then turn it round about the centre cross to find the number of positions (order of rotation) in which each shape looks the same.

Example

order of rotation = 4

①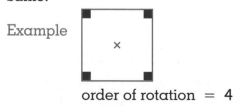

order of rotation =

②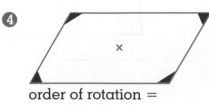

order of rotation =

③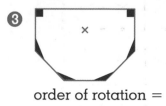

order of rotation =

④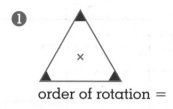

order of rotation =

⑤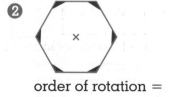

order of rotation =

⑥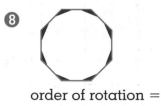

order of rotation =

⑦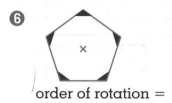

order of rotation =

⑧

order of rotation =

⑨

order of rotation =

D Use worksheet (11) to rotate these shapes around the marked cross and draw the image. Use tracing paper to help.

Example

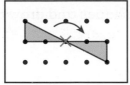

rotate $\frac{1}{2}$ turn

 ①

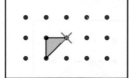

rotate 90° clockwise

 ②

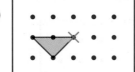

rotate 90° clockwise

 ③

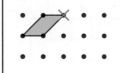

rotate 90° anti-clockwise

 ④

rotate 180° clockwise

⑤

rotate $\frac{1}{2}$ turn

⑥

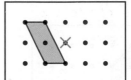

rotate $\frac{1}{4}$ turn clockwise

⑦

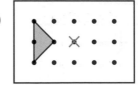

rotate $\frac{1}{4}$ turn anti-clockwise

⑧

rotate 180°

⑨

rotate $\frac{1}{2}$ turn

Translation

E Use worksheet (12) to translate these shapes and draw the new image.

Example

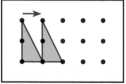

translate 1 unit right

1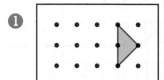

translate 2 units left

6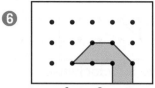

translate 2 units up

2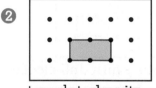

translate 1 unit up

7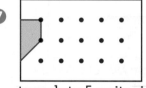

translate 5 units right

3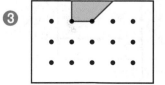

translate 2 units down

8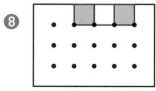

translate 2 units down

4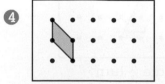

translate 3 units right

9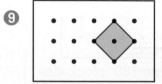

translate 3 units left

5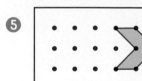

translate 4 units left

Congruence

F Use tracing paper to find out which shapes in the panel are congruent to the shaded shape.

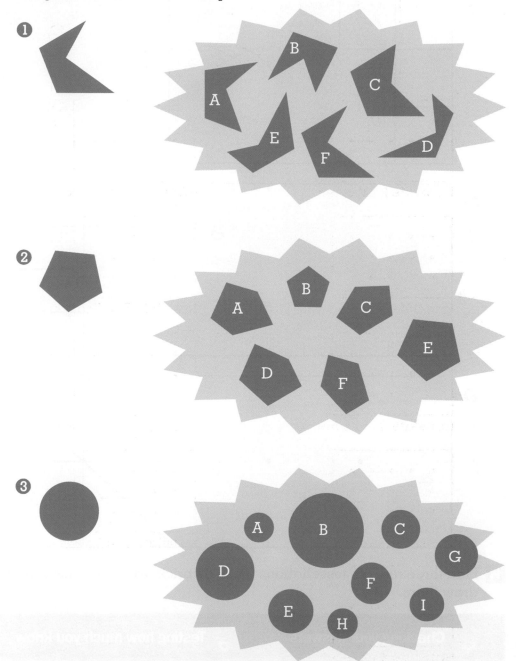

Tessellations

G Use worksheet (13) to complete each of the tessellations.

1

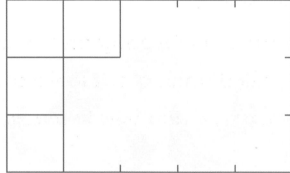

2

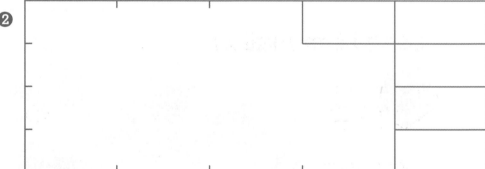

3

H Find three real-life tessellations (such as brick walls, floor tiles) and draw them.

 Checking your answers   **Testing how much you know**

Angles

This chapter is about measuring an amount of turn. This is called an angle. It looks at the different types of angle and how to measure and draw them.

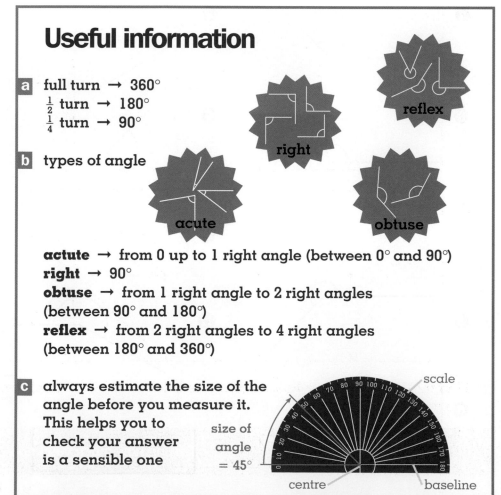

Useful information

a full turn → 360°
$\frac{1}{2}$ turn → 180°
$\frac{1}{4}$ turn → 90°

reflex

right

b types of angle

acute

obtuse

actute → from 0 up to 1 right angle (between 0° and 90°)
right → 90°
obtuse → from 1 right angle to 2 right angles
(between 90° and 180°)
reflex → from 2 right angles to 4 right angles
(between 180° and 360°)

c always estimate the size of the angle before you measure it. This helps you to check your answer is a sensible one

size of angle = 45°

scale

centre

baseline

Types of Angle

A Roughly draw each of these angles and write down if the angle is acute, obtuse, reflex or a right angle.

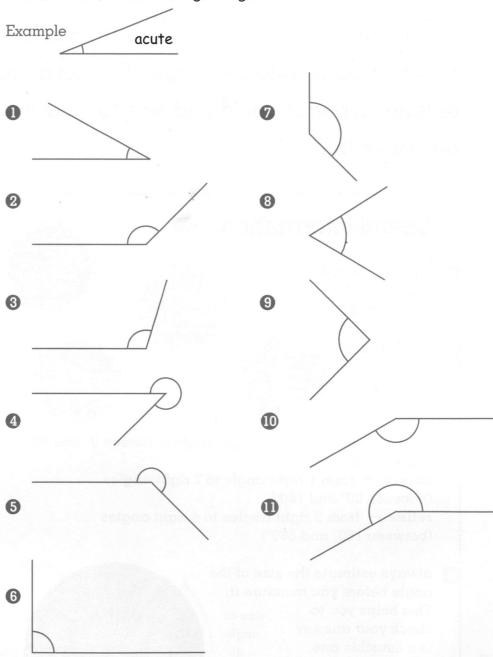

Example   acute

❶

❷

❸

❹

❺

❻

❼

❽

❾

❿

⓫

B Roughly draw each of these angles. Label each in turn as clockwise or anticlockwise.

clockwise

Example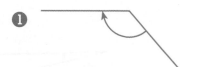

❶

❷

❸

❹

❺

❻

❼

❽

❾

❿

⓫

⓬

⓭

Measuring Angles

C Using worksheet (14) estimate, then carefully measure each angle and write down the answer.

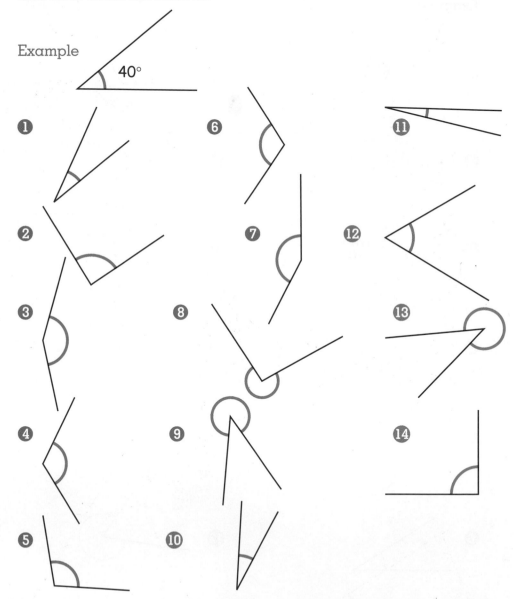

Example

40°

① ⑥ ⑪

② ⑦ ⑫

③ ⑧ ⑬

④ ⑨ ⑭

⑤ ⑩

D On worksheet (14) label each angle as larger than, smaller than or equal to a right angle.
Example *smaller than a right angle*

E Using worksheet (15) measure each of the angles and complete the table on the worksheet.

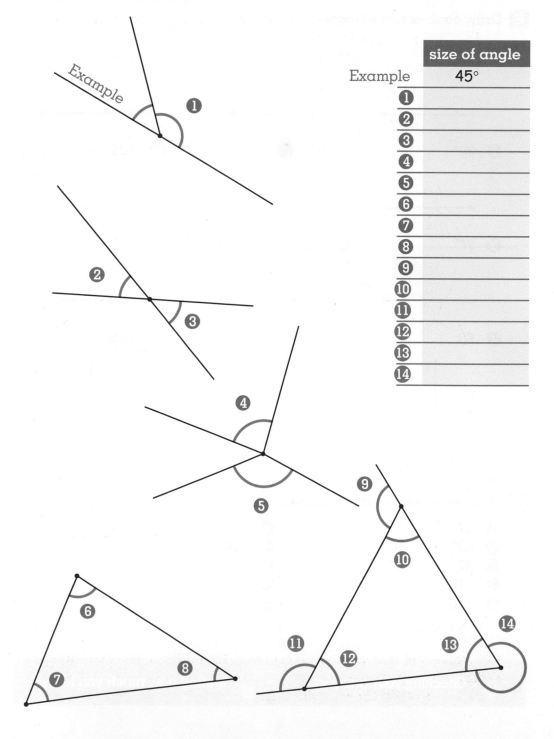

	size of angle
Example	45°
①	
②	
③	
④	
⑤	
⑥	
⑦	
⑧	
⑨	
⑩	
⑪	
⑫	
⑬	
⑭	

Drawing Angles

F Draw each of these angles.

1 40°   **5** 10°   **9** 170°

2 20°   **6** 85°   **10** 125°

3 70°   **7** 110°   **11** 105°

4 60°   **8** 140°   **12** 155°

G Now draw each of these angles.

1 37°   **6** 192°
2 52°   **7** 228°
3 97°   **8** 291°
4 113°   **9** 307°
5 165°   **10** 346°

Checking your answers   Testing how much you know

Units 2

This chapter is about different units used for measuring length, weight and capacity, and the way in which we change from one unit to the other.

Useful information

a rules for changing units

10 mm = 1 cm	1000 g = 1 kg	1000 ml = 1 litre
100 cm = 1 m	1000 kg = 1 tonne	100 cl = 1 litre
1000 m = 1 km		

b to add or take away mixed unit numbers you may find it easier to change them all into the same units

e.g.
3 cm + 20 mm = 3 cm + 2 cm = 5 cm

                or

           = 30 mm + 20 mm = 50 mm

Ch 9 Units 1

27 Multiply 10, Divide 10
EXTENSION: E12

Units of Length

A Copy and complete each of these questions.
Example 10 mm = 1 cm

1 30 mm = ___ cm
2 ___ mm = 5 cm
3 100 mm = ___ cm
4 ___ mm = 15 cm
5 ___ mm = 20 cm

6 45 mm = ___ cm
7 ___ mm = 2.5 cm
8 500 mm = ___ cm
9 76 mm = ___ cm

B Copy and complete each of these questions.
Example 1000 m = 1 km

1 ___ m = 2 km
2 4000 m = ___ km
3 1500 m = ___ km
4 ___ m = 6.5 km
5 3600 m = ___ km

6 500m = ___ km
7 ___ m = 0.2 cm
8 7600 m = ___ km
9 10 500 m = ___ km

C Copy the table. Use the map of the model railway to complete the table.

journey		centimetres	metres
Example	London → Bristol	70 + 40 = 110	1.1 m
1	London → Manchester		1.4 m
2	Norwich → Southampton		
3	Southampton → Birmingham		
4	London → Newcastle		
5	Brighton → Norwich		
6	Norwich → Birmingham		
7	Bristol → Liverpool		
8	Newcastle → Bristol		
9	Liverpool → Newcastle		

D Copy the table. Use the map of Swansea to complete the table.

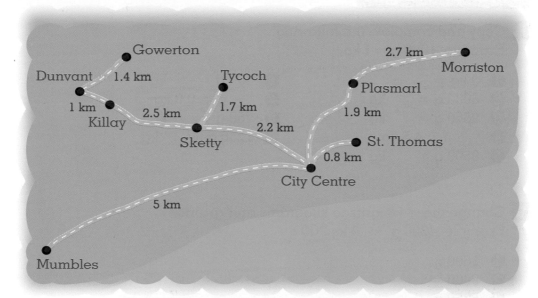

journey		kilometres	metres
Example	Mumbles → St. Thomas	5 + 0.8 = 5.8	5800
❶	Killay → City Centre		
❷	City Centre → Morriston		
❸	Gowerton → Killay		
❹	Dunvant → Tycoch		
❺	St. Thomas → Morriston		
❻	Plasmarl → Killay		
❼	Gowerton → Tycoch		
❽	Killay → Mumbles		
❾	Dunvant → Plasmarl		

E By changing all the lengths into the same units, work out these questions.
   Example 10 mm + 4 cm = 1 cm + 4 cm = 5 cm or 10 mm + 40 mm = 50 mm

❶ 20 mm + 20 cm =   ❺ 1 m + 17 cm =
❷ 40 mm + 12 cm =   ❻ 170 cm + 3 m =
❸ 15 cm – 70 mm =   ❼ 5 m – 200 cm =
❹ 2 cm – 10 mm =   ❽ 4 m – 150 cm =

Units of Weight

F Copy and complete the following.
Example 1000 g = 1 kg

❶ 3 kg = ___ g
❷ 5000 g = ___ kg
❸ 2500 g = ___ kg
❹ ___ g = 4.5 kg
❺ 6500 g = ___ kg

❻ 500 g = ___ kg
❼ ___ g = 0.3 kg
❽ 750 g = ___ kg
❾ 1250 g = ___ kg

G Change these weights to kilograms and grams.
Example 4200 g ⇒ 4 kg 200 g

❶ 1600 g
❷ 3800 g
❸ 5250 g
❹ 7829 g
❺ 10 340 g

H Change these weights into grams.
Example 2 kg 750 g ⇒ 2750g

❶ 1 kg 210 g
❷ 4 kg 930 g
❸ 3 kg 135 g
❹ 6 kg 987 g
❺ 9 kg 208 g

I Using the weights shown in the panel, show five ways to make exactly 1 kg.
Example 1 kg ⇒ 500 g + 250 g + 200 g+ 50 g

500 g   100 g
200 g   50 g
250 g   100 g   500 g
50 g   250 g
100 g

J Find the total of these weights in grams.

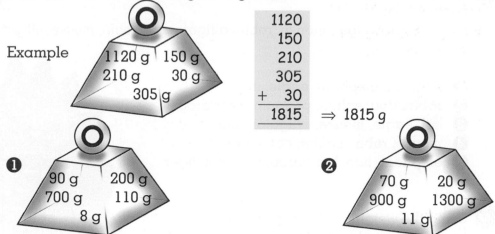

Example

1120 g 150 g
210 g   30 g
      305 g

```
  1120
   150
   210
   305
+   30
  1815   ⇒ 1815 g
```

❶

90 g   200 g
700 g   110 g
     8 g

❷

70 g   20 g
900 g   1300 g
     11 g

K Add together the weights shown in each bubble.

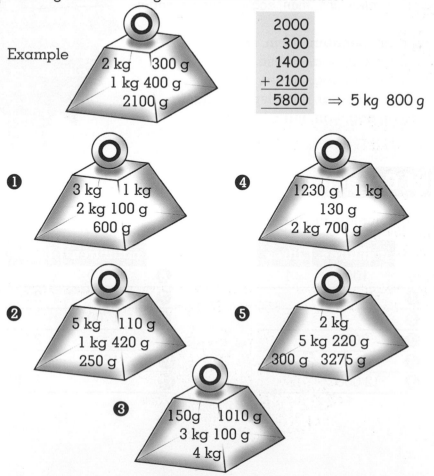

Example

2 kg   300 g
1 kg 400 g
   2100 g

```
  2000
   300
  1400
+ 2100
  5800   ⇒ 5 kg  800 g
```

❶

3 kg   1 kg
2 kg 100 g
   600 g

❹

1230 g   1 kg
      130 g
   2 kg 700 g

❷

5 kg   110 g
1 kg 420 g
   250 g

❺

      2 kg
   5 kg 220 g
300 g   3275 g

❸

150g   1010 g
   3 kg 100 g
      4 kg

L Using the weights in the panel, put the creatures in order of weight, lightest first.
Example lion, tiger, mouse, robin, alligator ⇒ robin, mouse, alligator, tiger, lion

1. lion, cat, elephant, eagle, man
2. robin, dog, spider, penguin, kangaroo
3. cat, eagle, mouse, alligator, dog
4. mouse, robin, spider, cat, eagle
5. elephant, lion, kangaroo, alligator, tiger

M Using the weights in the panel, put the creatures in order of weight, heaviest first.
Example robin, man, penguin, eagle, elephant ⇒ elephant, man, eagle, penguin, robin

1. dog, man, penguin, robin, spider
2. lion, tiger, cat, dog, mouse
3. mouse, eagle, dog, spider, robin
4. penguin, alligator, cat, elephant, tiger
5. alligator, dog, lion, man, kangaroo

spider → 10 g
lion → 120 kg
tiger → 94 kg
man → 80 kg
mouse → 260 g
penguin → 1900 g
robin → 120 g
cat → 1500 g
dog → 4 kg
elephant → 1500 kg
eagle → 2 kg
kangaroo → 50 kg
alligator → 70 kg

Units of Capacity

N Copy and complete the tables.

	millilitres	litres
Example	1000	1
1	3000	
2		5
3	9000	
4		10
5	12 000	

	millilitres	litres
6	500	
7		2.5
8	1700	
9		3.2
10	1270	
11		1.78

O Copy and complete the tables.

	centilitres	litres
Example	100	1
1	300	
2		4
3	900	
4		11
5	1200	

	centilitres	litres
6		1.5
7	50	
8		3.1
9	120	
10	260	
11		7.2

P Add the capacities shown in each jug.

Example

```
  300
   40
   12
+ 200
─────
  552    ⇒ 552 cl
```

1

2 l
8 cl
45 cl
170 cl

4

310 cl
4 l
4 cl
88 cl

2

3 l
7 cl
52 cl
120 cl

5

195 cl
24 cl
3 cl
1 l

3

16 cl
202 cl
6 cl
5 l

c working with decimals for multiplying and dividing (×, ÷), don't forget to keep the decimal point in your answer. Use 'carrying' as you do in all × and ÷ calculations

e.g.   £2.45 × 3

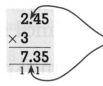

       2.45
    × 3
      7.35   ⟩ decimal point kept in the answer
      1 1

e.g   £25.60 ÷ 5

       5.12
   5) 25.60   ⟩ decimal point kept in the answer

Reading Decimal Scales

A What numbers do the arrows point to on each scale?
Example ⟹ 1.32 m

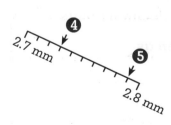

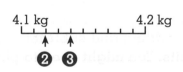

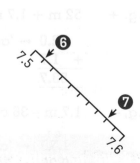

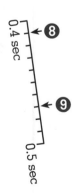

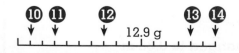

B What numbers do the arrows point to on these scales?

Example ⟹ 3.23 m

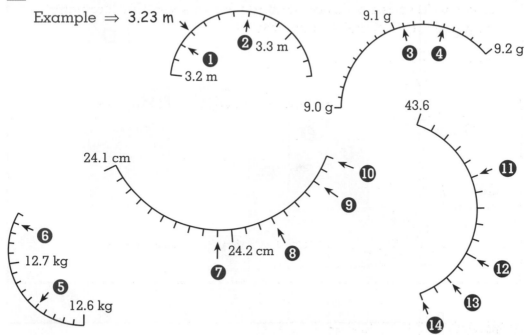

C The end of each object and scale is shown. The other end of the object is at the start of the scale. How long is each object?

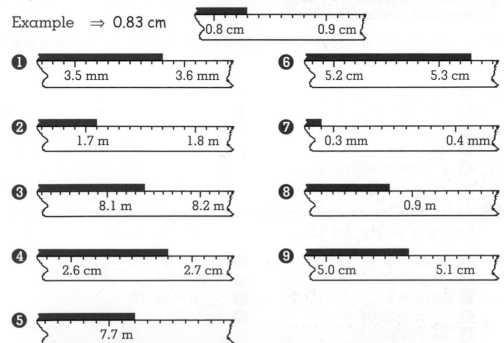

D How high is each block?

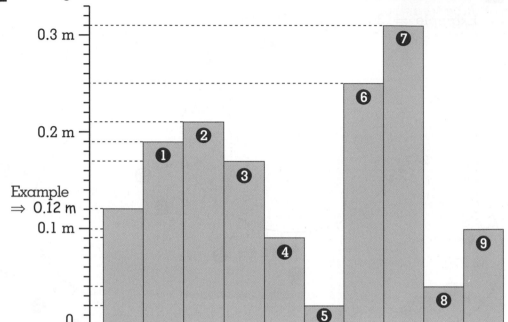

Changing Decimals

E As 100 cm is 1 m, copy and complete each of these questions in metres.
Example 110 cm = 1.1 m

1. 350 cm = ___ m
2. 263 cm = ___ m
3. ___ cm = 4.31 m
4. 307 cm = ___ m
5. ___ cm = 5.02 m

6. 2 m 17 cm = ___ m
7. 1 m 92 cm = ___ m
8. 3 m 4 cm = ___ m
9. ___ m ___ cm = 6.09 m

F As 100p is £1, copy and complete each of these questions in pounds (£).
Example 452p = £4.52

1. 330p = £ ___
2. ___p = £2.70
3. 107p = £ ___
4. ___p = £2.04
5. £1 + 53p = £ ___

6. £5 + 41p = £ ___
7. 67p = £ ___
8. ___p = £0.37
9. 8p = £ ___

G Match the lengths in panel A with the same lengths in panel B, and write them out.
Example 307 cm = 3.07 m

	A		B
	Example 307 cm		1.11 m
1	1 m 1 cm		3.70 m
2	3 m 70 cm		7.03 m
3	2 m 17 cm		2.71 m
4	1 m 10 cm		2.07 m
5	7 m 3 cm		7.30 m
6	271 cm		3.07 m
7	111 cm		1.10 m
8	730 cm		2.17 m
9	2 m 7 cm		1.01 m

Adding and Subtracting Decimals

H Copy and complete.

Example
```
  2.7
- 1.3
------
  1.4
```

1
```
  4.8
+ 3.1
-----
```

2
```
  5.4
- 2.3
-----
```

3
```
  3.4
+ 1.9
-----
```

4
```
  4.2
- 1.5
-----
```

5
```
  4.0
+ 1.8
-----
```

6
```
  5.0
- 2.7
-----
```

7
```
  3.0
- 1.6
-----
```

8
```
  7.6
+ 7.5
-----
```

I By setting out each of these questions in columns, work out the missing length.

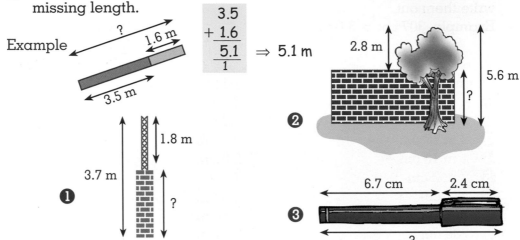

Example

$$\begin{array}{r} 3.5 \\ + 1.6 \\ \hline 5.1 \\ \hline 1 \end{array}$$ ⇒ 5.1 m

① 3.7 m, 1.8 m, ?

② 2.8 m, 5.6 m, ?

③ 6.7 cm, 2.4 cm, ?

J Set these questions out in columns to work out:

Example 2.23 + 1.45 ⇒ $$\begin{array}{r} 2.23 \\ +1.45 \\ \hline 3.68 \end{array}$$

① 6.05 + 1.41
② 4.27 + 3.55
③ 1.58 + 2.74
④ 5.64 − 2.32

⑤ 8.99 − 5.45
⑥ 7.21 − 4.16
⑦ 3.52 − 1.71
⑧ 6.35 − 3.49

K How much longer is the longer piece of wood in each question? Show your calculations.

Example

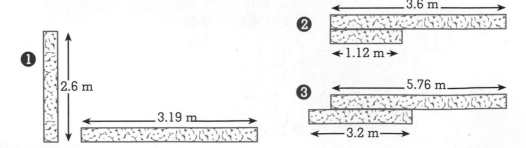

1.5 m
2.36 m

$$\begin{array}{r} ^{1\ 1}\\ 2.36 \\ - 1.50 \\ \hline 0.86 \end{array}$$ ⇒ 0.86 m

① 2.6 m, 3.19 m

② 3.6 m, 1.12 m

③ 5.76 m, 3.2 m

L Find the total length for each of the questions. Show your calculations.

Example

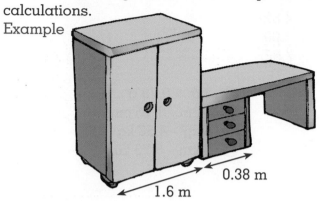

```
  1.60
+ 0.38
  1.98
```
⇒ 1.98 m

0.38 m

1.6 m

❶

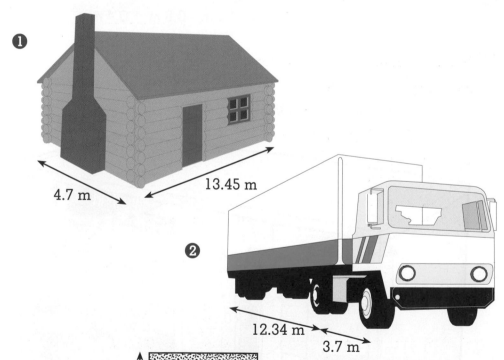

4.7 m

13.45 m

❷

12.34 m

3.7 m

❸

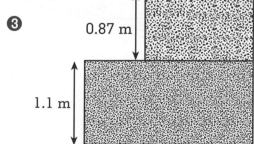

0.87 m

1.1 m

171

M By setting out in columns, work out these questions.

Example 4.62 + 3 $\Rightarrow$

$$\begin{array}{r} 4.62 \\ +\ 3.00 \\ \hline 7.62 \end{array}$$

1 8.75 + 4
2 5.51 − 2
3 6 + 1.74
4 5 m + 2.36 m

5 8 g + 0.79 g
6 7 cm − 1.25 cm
7 6 kg − 4.56 kg
8 9 km − 8.73 km

N Find the difference in height between:
Example book and coffee jar $\Rightarrow$ 1.2 m − 0.8 m = 0.4 m

1 oil and flour packet
2 mats and biscuit tin
3 book and biscuit tin
4 coffee jar and flour packet
5 book and oil container

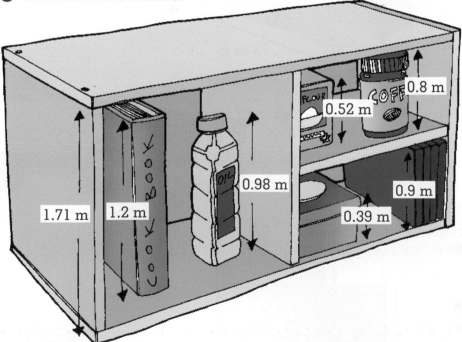

O Find the sum of the numbers in each bubble.

Example

$$\begin{array}{r} 1.1 \\ 2.3 \\ 4.2 \\ 1.0 \\ + \;\; 8.1 \\ \hline 16.7 \end{array}$$

❶ 1.1 3.0
3.8
4.8 5.1

❺ 2.4 3.6
6.5
4.2 5.3

❾ 1.6 2.7
5.6
3.3 4.4

❷ 2.0 2.9
3.9
4.1 5.2

❻ 3.7 4.7
2.3
1.2 6.1

❿ 2.5 1.8
5.5
3.2 4.3

❸ 4.5 2.6
3.4
5.0 1.4

❼ 1.5 2.1
5.7
3.1 4.6

❹ 1.7 2.8
6.0
3.5 5.4

❽ 2.2 6.3
1.3
4.0 5.8

Multiplying and Dividing Decimals

P Work out these questions and then check the answers on a calculator.
Example if a book costs £3.75,
how much do 3 of those books cost? ⇒

$$\begin{array}{r} £3.75 \\ \times \quad\;\; 3 \\ \hline £11.25 \\ {\scriptstyle 2\;\;1} \end{array}$$

❶ If a bottle of wine costs £2.15, how much does a box of 6 bottles cost?

❷ If a man earns £4.80 an hour, how much does he earn in 4 hours?

Q Work out these questions and then check the answers on a calculator.
Example A group of 4 friends wins £16.60 in a raffle. How much do
they get each if it is shared equally? ⇒

$$4\overline{)16.60} = 4.15 \Rightarrow £4.15$$

with quotient 4.15 above and small 2 below.

1 If 4 people equally share £3.00, how much do they each get?
(Hint: change £3 into 300p.)

2 If 3 brothers are given £11.40 to share equally at Christmas, how
much are they each given?

3 This piece of wood is divided into 3 equal pieces. Find the length
of each piece

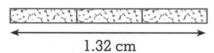

1.32 cm

4 These 2 books of identical thickness are stacked on top of each
other. How thick is each book?

1.32 cm

5 When 4 girls buy a large chococlate bar, it costs £0.96. If they
share the cost equally, how much does each girl pay?

Checking your answers   Testing how much you know

Time 1

This chapter is about telling the time using clockfaces and about using time-lines and calendars.

Useful information

a clockfaces

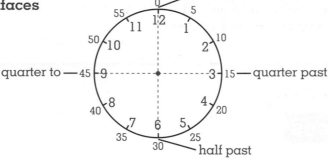

numbers on the inside of this clockface show **hours**
numbers on the outside show **minutes** (these numbers are not really on the clockface)

b changing units

60 seconds → 1 minute
60 minutes → 1 hour
24 hours → 1 day
7 days → 1 week

c timelines

7 pm	7.30 pm	8 pm	8.30 pm

marked every 15 minutes

4 am	4.30 am	5 am

marked every 10 minutes

Ch 22 Units 2

Ch 35 Time 2
5 Graphs and Tables 2

ORKSHEET: W16, W17

c the months of the year are:

1	January	7	July
2	February	8	August
3	March	9	September
4	April	10	October
5	May	11	November
6	June	12	December

d a calendar

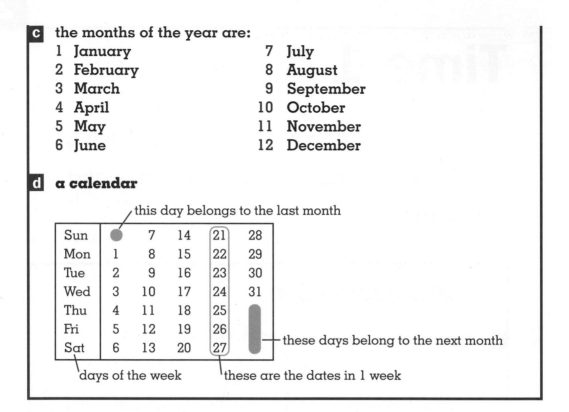

this day belongs to the last month

Sun	●	7	14	21	28
Mon	1	8	15	22	29
Tue	2	9	16	23	30
Wed	3	10	17	24	31
Thu	4	11	18	25	
Fri	5	12	19	26	
Sat	6	13	20	27	

these days belong to the next month

days of the week

these are the dates in 1 week

Clockfaces

A Write down the time shown on these clockfaces.

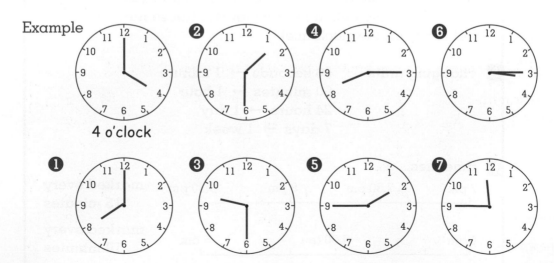

Example

4 o'clock

B Write down the time shown on these clockfaces.

Example

2:05

❷

❹

❻

❶

❸

❺

❼

C How many minutes past the hour is shown on each clock?

Example

3 minutes past

❷

❹

❶

❸

❺

D How many minutes past the hour is shown on each clock?

Example

32 minutes past

❷

❹

❶

❸

❺

Answer sections **E** – **H** on worksheets (17) and (18).

E Draw these times onto clockfaces.
Example 1 o'clock

❶ 10 o'clock   ❻ 11 o'clock
❷ 6 o'clock   ❼ 7 o'clock
❸ 4 o'clock   ❽ 5 o'clock
❹ 9 o'clock   ❾ 12 o'clock
❺ 2 o'clock

F Draw these times onto clockfaces.
Example half past 3

❶ half past 7   ❻ 4 thirty
❷ 2 thirty   ❼ half past 6
❸ 11 thirty   ❽ 8 thirty
❹ half past 1   ❾ 9:30
❺ half past 12

G Draw these times onto clockfaces.
Example quarter past 7

❶ quarter past 11   ❻ 5 fifteen
❷ 2 fifteen   ❼ quarter past 9
❸ quarter past 3   ❽ 1:15
❹ 8 fifteen   ❾ 10:15
❺ quarter past 4

H Draw these times onto clockfaces.
Example quarter to 2

❶ quarter to 10   ❻ 6 forty-five
❷ 3 forty-five   ❼ quarter to 12
❸ quarter to 8   ❽ 1:45
❹ 7 forty-five   ❾ 5:45
❺ quarter to 4

I Change these written times into times in numbers.
Example quarter past two ⇒ 2.15

❶ half past seven   ❹ quarter to twelve
❷ quarter past five   ❺ half past eleven
❸ quarter to eight   ❻ quarter past one

J Change these times in numbers into written times.
Example 8.45 ⇒ quarter to nine

❶ 1.30   ❹ 11.15
❷ 3.45   ❺ 5.30
❸ 9.15   ❻ 1.45

K What will be the time 10 minutes after the times shown below?

Example

3:10

❷    ❹    ❻

❶    ❸    ❺    ❼

L What was the time 20 minutes before the times shown below?

Example

11 o'clock

❷    ❹

❶    ❸    ❺   ❼

179

Changing Time

M Change each of these into seconds (s), minutes (min) or minutes and seconds.

Example 60 s $\Rightarrow$ 1 min 0 s

➊ 120 s $\Rightarrow$ ___ min ___ s
➋ 4 min 0 s $\Rightarrow$ ___ s
➌ 180 s $\Rightarrow$ ___ min ___ s
➍ 300 s $\Rightarrow$ ___ min ___ s
➎ 1min 30 s $\Rightarrow$ ___ s
➏ 100 s $\Rightarrow$ ___ min ___ s

➐ 6 min 0 s $\Rightarrow$ ___ s
➑ 2 min 40 s $\Rightarrow$ ___ s
➒ 135 s $\Rightarrow$ ___ min ___ s
➓ 4 min 50 s $\Rightarrow$ ___ s
⓫ 200 s $\Rightarrow$ ___ min ___ s

N Change each of these into minutes (min), hours (hr) or hours and minutes.

Example 120 min $\Rightarrow$ 2 hr 0 min

➊ 60 min $\Rightarrow$ ___ hr ___ min
➋ 3 hr 0 min $\Rightarrow$ ___ min
➌ 1 hr 10 min $\Rightarrow$ ___ min
➍ 240 min $\Rightarrow$ ___ hr ___ min
➎ 80 min $\Rightarrow$ ___ hr ___ min

➏ 2 hr 45 min $\Rightarrow$ ___ min
➐ 95 min $\Rightarrow$ ___ hr ___ min
➑ 3 hr 20 min $\Rightarrow$ ___ min
➒ 4 hr 10 min $\Rightarrow$ ___ min
➓ 150 min $\Rightarrow$ ___ hr ___ min

O Change each of these into weeks and days or days only.

Example 10 days $\Rightarrow$ 1 week 3 days

➊ 7 days $\Rightarrow$ ___ weeks ___ days
➋ 2 weeks 0 days $\Rightarrow$ ___ days
➌ 12 days $\Rightarrow$ ___ weeks ___ days
➍ 1 week 6 days $\Rightarrow$ ___ days
➎ 2 weeks 4 days $\Rightarrow$ ___ days
➏ 15 days $\Rightarrow$ ___ weeks ___ days
➐ 22 days $\Rightarrow$ ___ weeks ___ days
➑ 3 weeks 4 days $\Rightarrow$ ___ days
➒ 6 weeks 1 day $\Rightarrow$ ___ days
➓ 34 days $\Rightarrow$ ___ weeks ___ days

Timelines

P Use the timeline to find the length of time, in minutes or hours from:
Example C → D ⇒ 15 minutes

9 am 9.15   9.30   9.45 10 am   10.30   11 am   11.30   12 am

A   B   C   D   E   F

1 A → B
2 C → E
3 D → F
4 B → C
5 B → D

6 A → D
7 C → F
8 B → F
9 A → F

Q Use the timeline to write, in minutes or hours, the time from:
Example B → C ⇒ 10 minutes

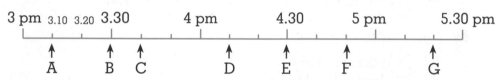

3 pm 3.10 3.20 3.30   4 pm   4.30   5 pm   5.30 pm

A   B   C   D   E   F   G

1 A → B
2 B → D
3 B → E
4 D → F
5 E → G

6 D → G
7 B → F
8 A → F
9 A → G

R Use the timeline to write, in minutes or hours, the time from:
Example B → C ⇒ 10 minutes

7 pm   7.30   8 pm   8.30

A   B   C   D   E   F

1 D → E
2 B → D
3 A → D

4 B → E
5 A → E

Calendars

S Answer the questions about the calendar below.

Sun		7	14	21	28
Mon	1	8	15	22	29
Tues	2	9	16	23	
Wed	3	10	17	24	
Thurs	4	11	18	25	
Fri	5	12	19	26	
Sat	6	13	20	27	

February

Sun		6	13	20	27
Mon		7	14	21	28
Tues	1	8	15	22	29
Wed	2	9	16	23	30
Thur	3	10	17	24	31
Fri	4	11	18	25	
Sat	5	12	19	26	

March

Sun		3	10	17	24
Mon		4	11	18	25
Tues		5	12	19	26
Wed		6	13	20	27
Thurs		7	14	21	28
Fri	1	8	15	22	29
Sat	2	9	16	23	30

April

❶ What days of the week are these dates?
Example 6 February? ⇒ Saturday

(a) 10 March

(b) 13 April

(c) 24 February

(d) 28 March

(e) 30 April

(f) 11 April

❷ How many:

(a) Sundays in February?

(b) Thursdays in March?

(c) Saturdays in April?

❸ What date is:

(a) the first Thursday in February?

(b) the last Sunday in April?

(c) the second Saturday in March?

❹ Which of the months in the above calendar has:

(a) 5 Tuesdays?

(b) 5 Mondays?

(c) the 17th on a Thursday?

❺ What day of the week is:

(a) 2 days after 3 February?

(b) 3 days before 10 April?

(c) 5 days after 18 March?

T Copy out this rhyme.

> Thirty days has September
> April, June and November
> All the rest have thirty-one
> Except for February alone
> Which has twenty-eight days clear
> And twenty-nine in each leap year

❶ List the months of the year with 30 days

❷ List the months of the year with 31 days

❸ Copy and complete this sentence:

Once every 4 years February has an extra day and that year is call a _____ year.

❹ Work out how many days there are in total in:
Example January, March and August $\Rightarrow$ 31 + 31 + 31 = 93 days

   (a)   September, November and April

   (b)   June, August and May

   (c)   July, September and October

U Calculate the timespan in days between:
Example 4 March and 12 March $\Rightarrow$ 8 days

❶ 7 June and 15 June   **❸** 3 July and 19 July

❷ 5 May and 17 May   **❹** 1 August and 26 August

V Calculate the timespan in weeks and days between:
Example 16 May and 4 June $\Rightarrow$ 15 days to end of May + 4 days in June = 19 days = 2 weeks + 5 days

❶ 10 December and 3 January   **❸** 15 March and 22 April

❷ 26 June and 14 July   **❹** 14 August and 27 September

✓ **Checking your answers**   ❓ **Testing how much you know**

Graphs and Tables 2

This chapter is about drawing graphs and about finding information from tables and graphs.

Useful information

a always read questions carefully

b make sure you understand each table

c draw graphs with a pencil and ruler

d label each axis

e write a title above your graph

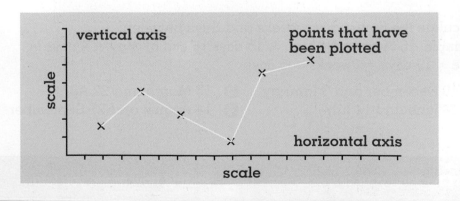

Ch 10 Graphs and Tables

Ch 35 Time 2

EXTENSION: E17, E18,

Holiday Information

A Use the table on train prices to work out the return fare for these journeys.

Example   1 adult to Birmingham $\Rightarrow$ £24

① 2 adults to Manchester
② 1 child to Cardiff
③ 1 adult and 1 child to Exeter
④ 2 children to Newcastle
⑤ 4 adults to Cardiff
⑥ 1 adult and 2 children to Southampton
⑦ 2 adults to Glasgow
⑧ 2 adults and 1 child to Manchester
⑨ 2 adults and 2 children to Birmingham

Return fares from London		
Destination	Adult	Child
Southampton	£27	£15
Birmingham	£24	£13
Manchester	£42	£20
Cardiff	£36	£19
Exeter	£33	£17
Newcastle	£48	£26
Glasgow	£59	£31

B Use the table in **A**. In these questions a railcard is used where children travel for £1 if travelling with an adult. Work out the cost of a return journey for:

① 1 adult and 1 child to Exeter
② 2 adults and 1 child to Manchester
③ 2 adults and 2 children to Birmingham

Use this table with sections **C**, **D** and **E**

Return Fares from London						
Destination	Before 9.30 am			After 9.30 am		
	Adult	OAP	Child	Adult	OAP	Child
Gatwick	£15	£10	£8	£13	£9	£7
Heathrow	£12	£9	£7	£10	£8	£6
Luton	£14	£10	£8	£12	£9	£7
Swindon	£21	£13	£11	£18	£11	£10
Norwich	£28	£17	£15	£25	£15	£13
Portsmouth	£19	£12	£10	£17	£10	£8

C Write down the return fares for:
Example 1 adult to Heathrow before 9.30 am ⇒ £12

① 1 OAP to Luton after 9.30 am
② 1 child to Swindon after 9.30 am
③ 2 adults to Portsmouth before 9.30 am
④ 2 adults to Portsmouth after 9.30 am
⑤ 1 adult and 1 child to Norwich before 9.30 am
⑥ 1 OAP and 1 child to Gatwick before 9.30 am
⑦ 4 OAPs to Heathrow after 9.30 am
⑧ 2 adults and 1 child to Swindon after 9.30 am
⑨ 2 adults, 2 children and 1 OAP to Heathrow before 9.30 am

D To reserve a seat on the train costs £1 each. Work out the cost for
each of the above journeys **C** , questions ① – ⑨, if every person has
reserved a seat.
Example 1 adult to Heathrow before 9.30 am ⇒ £13

E Using a railcard (where each child travels for £1) work out the cost
of the fares for:

① 2 adults and 1 child to Swindon before 9.30 am
② 2 adults and 1 child to Swindon after 9.30 am
③ 2 adults and 2 children to Luton before 9.30 am
④ 3 adults and 3 children to Heathrow after 9.30 am
⑤ 4 adults and 4 children to Gatwick after 9.30 am

Use this hotel price list for sections **F** and **G**

	Room type	Length of stay			
		1 night	Short break (3 nights)	1 week	2 weeks
Nov–April	Single	£30	£ 75	£180	£330
	Double	£36	£ 90	£216	£396
	Family	£45	£112	£270	£495
May–Oct.	Single	£40	£100	£240	£440
	Double	£48	£120	£288	£528
	Family	£60	£150	£360	£660

Prices are per room not per person

Evening meal + £6 each person

F Work out the cost of:
Example a single room for 1 night in May ⇒ £40

❶ a double room for 1 night in December
❷ a family room for 2 nights in March
❸ a double room for 1 week in August
❹ a single room for 2 weeks in January
❺ a family room for 3 nights in June
❻ 2 single rooms for 1 night in September
❼ a family room for 2 weeks in October
❽ 2 double rooms for 1 week in July
❾ 2 family rooms for 3 nights in January

G If an evening meal is also taken, work out the cost of:

❶ 2 adults in a double room for 1 night in May
❷ 2 adults in single rooms for 1 night in May
❸ 1 adult in a single room for 1 week in February
❹ 2 adults in a double room for 3 nights in April
❺ 2 adults and 2 children in a family room for 3 nights in August

Supermarket Information

H The graph shows the number of chickens sold each day in one week.
Copy and complete the table.

Day	Mon	Tues	Wed	Thurs	Fri	Sat	Sun
Example chickens sold	7						

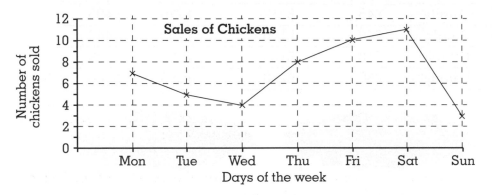

1 On which day were most chickens sold?
2 On which day were fewest chickens sold?
3 How many chickens were sold altogether?

I This graph shows how many boxes of washing powder were sold
each day. Copy and complete the table.

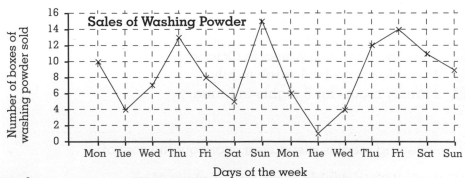

Example

Day	Mon	Tues	Wed	Thurs	Fri	Sat	Sun	Mon	Tues	Wed	Thurs	Fri	Sat	Sun
powder sold	10													

J Copy and complete the graph showing the number of bottles of cola sold each day.

Day	Mon	Tues	Wed	Thurs	Fri	Sat	Sun
Cola sold	4	1	7	2	9	8	3

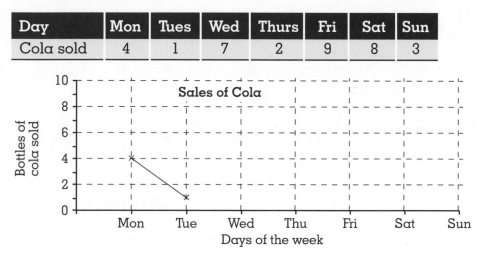

K Use this table to draw a graph showing the number of packets of cereal sold each day for a fortnight.

Day and Date	Mon 10 May	Tue 11 May	Wed 12 May	Thurs 13 May	Fri 14 May	Sat 15 May	Sun 16 May	Mon 17 May	Tue 18 may	Wed 19 May	Thurs 20 May	Fri 21 May	Sat 22 May	Sun 23 May
cereal sold	12	7	9	3	1	0	14	10	3	8	4	11	13	6

Answer these questions

1. On which day was most cereal sold?
2. On which dates were the same amounts of cereal sold?
3. How many packets of cereal were sold in the first week?
4. How many packets of cereal were sold in the second week?

L A baby shop's three best-selling items are shown on this graph. Copy and complete the table below.

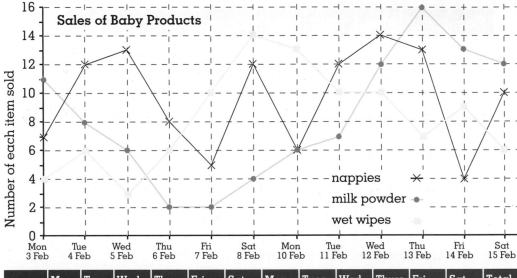

Item	Mon 3 Feb	Tues 4 Feb	Wed 5 Feb	Thurs 6 Feb	Fri 7 Feb	Sat 8 Feb	Mon 10 Feb	Tues 11 Feb	Wed 12 Feb	Thurs 13 Feb	Fri 14 Feb	Sat 15 Feb	Total per item
Nappies	7												
Wet Wipes	4												
Milk Powder	11												
												Total all items=	

M From the table in **L** find:

1. how many nappies were sold altogether
2. how much milk powder was sold in the first week
3. how many wet wipes were sold in the second week
4. how many nappies were sold on the second Wednesday
5. the total sales for the first Friday
6. on which day most milk powder was sold
7. on which day the fewest nappies were sold
8. which 2 days in a row had the same sales of wet wipes

 Checking your answers   **Testing how much you know**

Chance

This chapter is about the words we use to describe the chance of something happening.

Useful information

a   **certain**: must happen
impossible: will never happen
uncertain: could happen
likely: good chance of happening
unlikely: little chance of happening
even: exactly half or 50-50 chance of happening
fair: you are made to think each thing has the same chance of happening, and this is right
unfair: you are made to think each thing has the same chance of happening, but this is wrong

b

impossible   even   certain

←—— gets less likely   gets more likely ——→

EXTENSION: E20

From Impossible to Certain

A Write whether each event is certain or impossible.
Example night follows day $\Rightarrow$ certain

1. you will live forever
2. a man will jump over Big Ben
3. adding 4 to 2 will give 6
4. taking 6 from 10 will give 5

B Write if each event is certain, uncertain or impossible.
Example Tuesday follows Monday $\Rightarrow$ certain

1. you will get married
2. 30 minutes makes an hour
3. you will be a millionaire
4. you will cut your finger

C Write if each event is likely or unlikely.
Example you will visit Mars $\Rightarrow$ unlikely

1. you will go on holiday this year
2. it will be dry for most of July
3. you will have fish for tea
4. you will have children one day

D Copy out each list. Tick the most likely event and cross the most unlikely event.

Example a coin landing on heads ✓
a coin landing on its edge
a coin never landing ✗

1. the sun will shine this week
the sun will explode today
the sun will shine all this week

2. a die lands on 1
a die lands on an even number
a die lands on its edge

3. you will breathe today
you will fall over today
you will die today

E Put these lists in order, from the impossible to the certain.

❶
seven days make a week
the month ends in a Y
a coin lands on heads
7 + 4 = 12

❷
it will snow tomorrow
May follows June
12 months make a year
you will have homework tonight

❸
you will go on holiday this year
throw a 7 on a die
a coin lands on tails
the word TIME has an E in it

Even Chance?

F Write whether each of these events has an even chance, less than even chance or more than even chance of happening.
Example a 2 rolled on a die ⇒ *less than even chance*

❶ you will eat today
❷ a coin lands on tails
❸ a month begins with J
❹ an even number rolled on a die
❺ a die lands on 1, 2, 3 or 4
❻ an odd number rolled on a die
❼ you will watch TV this week
❽ a coin lands on heads
❾ a die lands on a 5

G Draw this scale and put labels on it to show the possibility for the events below.

impossible   unlikely   even   likely   certain

Example even ⇒ a coin lands on heads

1 Saturday comes before Sunday
2 you will grow an extra arm
3 pick a 2 of spades from a pack of cards
4 rolling an even number on a die

H Draw this scale and put labels on it to show the possibility for the events below.

unlikely   even   likely

less than even   more than even

1 you will be a pop singer
2 you will have cereal for breakfast
3 you will get married
4 it will be dry tomorrow
5 a coin will land on tails

Fair or Unfair?

I To be fair a die or coin should land *about* the same number of times on each of its faces or sides. Look at the tally tables of when a coin or die is rolled and say if they are fair or unfair.

Example

| heads | ЖЖ I |
| tails | ЖЖ |

⇒ fair

❶

| heads | ЖЖ ЖЖ III |
| tails | ЖЖ I |

❷

| heads | ЖЖ II |
| tails | ЖЖ ЖЖ ЖЖ III |

❸

1	IIII
2	II
3	IIIII
4	III
5	ЖЖ
6	III

❺

1	ЖЖ ЖЖ II
2	ЖЖ ЖЖ I
3	ЖЖ ЖЖ IIII
4	ЖЖ ЖЖ
5	ЖЖ ЖЖ III
6	ЖЖ ЖЖ II

❹

1	ЖЖ I
2	II
3	ЖЖ II
4	ЖЖ III
5	I
6	ЖЖ III

❻

1	ЖЖ ЖЖ II
2	I
3	
4	ЖЖ ЖЖ I
5	ЖЖ ЖЖ III
6	II

B Look carefully at your answers to **A** and work out how long 10 shapes of these lengths would be.
Example 0.7 cm $\Rightarrow$ 7 cm

1 1.3 cm

2 1.8 cm

3 2 cm

4 1.6 cm

5 2.1 cm

6 3.5 cm

7 4.7 cm

C Look at this section from the times tables. Work out these questions.
Example $2 \times 10 = 20$

1 $10 \times 3 =$

2 $5 \times 10 =$

3 $10 \times 7 =$

4 $4 \times 10 =$

5 $10 \times 6 =$

6 $8 \times 10 =$

7 $10 \times 9 =$

$8 \times 1 = 8$	$9 \times 1 = 9$	$10 \times 1 = 10$
$8 \times 2 = 16$	$9 \times 2 = 18$	$10 \times 2 = 20$
$8 \times 3 = 24$	$9 \times 3 = 27$	$10 \times 3 = 30$
$8 \times 4 = 32$	$9 \times 4 = 36$	$10 \times 4 = 40$
$8 \times 5 = 40$	$9 \times 5 = 45$	$10 \times 5 = 50$
$8 \times 6 = 48$	$9 \times 6 = 54$	$10 \times 6 = 60$
$8 \times 7 = 56$	$9 \times 7 = 63$	$10 \times 7 = 70$
	$9 \times 8 = 72$	$10 \times 8 = 80$

D When you multiply a whole number by 10, you add a zero.
Work out these questions.
Example $11 \times 10 = 110$

1 13×10

2 15×10

3 20×10

4 22×10

5 43×10

6 72×10

7 103×10

8 114×10

9 223×10

E When you multiply a whole number by 100, you add 2 zeros.
Write down the answer to these questions.
Example $2 \times 100 = 200$

1 6×100

2 12×100

3 14×100

4 21×100

5 30×100

6 67×100

7 88×100

8 107×100

9 276×100

F Look at the answers in the panel. All that has happened is that the decimal point has disappeared. Write down the answer to these questions.

Example $1.5 \times 10 = 15$

1 1.8×10 **5** 8.3×10

2 2.4×10 **6** 7.7×10

3 3.9×10 **7** 9.3×10

4 5.6×10

$1.1 \times 10 = 11$
$1.2 \times 10 = 12$
$1.3 \times 10 = 13$
$1.4 \times 10 = 14$
$1.5 \times 10 = 15$
$1.6 \times 10 = 16$

G To multiply *any* number by 10, you move the decimal point one space to the right. Work out these questions.

Example $4.37 \times 10 \Rightarrow 4.\overset{\frown}{3}7 = 43.7$

1 72.38×10 **5** 256.1×10

2 1.49×10 **6** 3.0502×10

3 2.365×10 **7** $56.0 \times 10 \; (56 \times 10)$

4 0.17×10 **8** 73.0×10

H To multiply *any* number by 100, you move the decimal point 2 spaces to the right. Work out these questions.

Example $3.25 \times 100 \Rightarrow 3.\overset{\frown\frown}{25} = 325$

1 14.62×100 **5** 800.42×100

2 7.613×100 **6** $43 \times 100 \; (43.00 \times 100)$

3 0.17×100 **7** 79×100

4 0.06×100 **8** 128×100

I Copy and complete.

Example

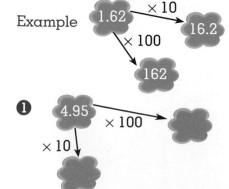

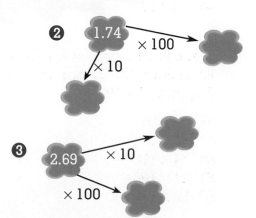

J Work out each of these questions. (Hint: the answers are all in the panel)

Example A book is 1.4 cm thick. Work out the thickness of 10 books

$\Rightarrow 1.\overset{\frown}{4} \times 10 = 14$ cm

❶ A cake costs 42p. Write down the cost of 10 identical cakes.

❷ A pen weighs 0.2 kg. Write down the weight of 10 pens.

❸ A window is 1.3 m wide. Work out the width of 10 of those windows.

❹ It takes 12.3 seconds to eat a biscuit. How long would it take to eat 10 biscuits?

❺ It takes 17 seconds to write one line, how long would it take to write 100 identical lines?

❻ A tile is 0.4 cm thick. Work out the thickness of 100 tiles.

❼ A piece of wood is 3.2 m long. If 100 identical pieces of wood were put end to end, work out the total length.

❽ A car is 4.6 m long. How long would 100 cars be when parked bumper to bumper?

❾ A flea is 0.03 cm wide. How wide would 100 fleas be standing side by side?

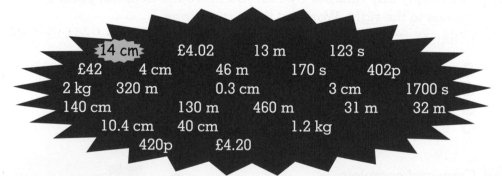

14 cm   £4.02   13 m   123 s
£42   4 cm   46 m   170 s   402p
2 kg   320 m   0.3 cm   3 cm   1700 s
140 cm   130 m   460 m   31 m   32 m
10.4 cm   40 cm   1.2 kg
420p   £4.20

Dividing by 10 and 100

K You are told the length of 10 shapes. Measure carefully the length of one shape.

①

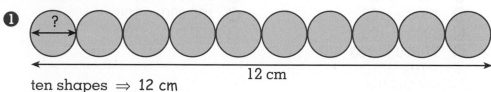

12 cm

ten shapes ⇒ 12 cm
one shape ⇒

②

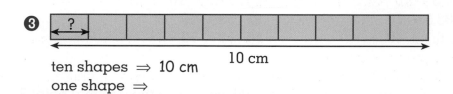

7 cm

ten shapes ⇒ 7 cm
one shape ⇒

③

?

10 cm

ten shapes ⇒ 10 cm
one shape ⇒

L Look carefully at your answes to **K** . If 10 shapes are the following lengths, find the length of 1 shape.
Example 8 cm ⇒ 0.8 cm

① 5 cm
② 9 cm
③ 12 cm
④ 17 cm

⑤ 21 cm
⑥ 33 cm
⑦ 41 cm

M When you divide a large number by 10, you cross off the last zero.
Copy and complete these questions.
Example 45̸0 ÷ 10 = 45

① 300 ÷ 10
② 490 ÷ 10
③ 680 ÷ 10
④ 4 200 ÷ 10
⑤ 6 780 ÷ 10

⑥ 9000 ÷ 10
⑦ 17 000 ÷ 10
⑧ 1 050 000 ÷ 10
⑨ 300 000 ÷ 10

N When you divide a large number by 100, you cross off the last 2 zeros.
Copy and complete these questions.
Example 4ØØ ÷ 100 = 4

1 700 ÷ 100
2 1500 ÷ 100
3 6000 ÷ 100
4 17 000 ÷ 100

5 20 000 ÷ 100
6 130 000 ÷ 100
7 400 000 ÷ 100

O When you divide *any* number by 10, you move the decimal point 1
space to the left. Work out the answer to these questions.
Example 13.7 ÷ 10 ⟹ 13.7 = 1.37

1 26.8 ÷ 10
2 74.5 ÷ 10
3 133.9 ÷ 10
4 206.1 ÷ 10

5 4327.4 ÷ 10
6 37.0 ÷ 10
7 59 ÷ 10
8 18 ÷ 10

P When you divide *any* number by 100, you move the decimal point 2
spaces to the left. Work out the answer to these questions.
Example 412.3 ÷ 100 ⟹ 412.3 = 4.123

1 129.81 ÷ 100
2 4357.2 ÷ 100
3 6000.5 ÷ 100

4 700 ÷ 100
5 326 ÷ 100
6 1832 ÷ 100

Q Work out the answer to these questions.

1 Divide out £550 among 100 children

2 A pile of 100 books is 132 cm high. How is high each one?

3 100 sweets weigh 741.3 g. How much does 1 weigh?

4 If you run 100 m in 15.3 seconds, how long did 1 m take to run?

✔ **Checking your answers**   ◉ **Testing how much you know**

Fractions

This chapter is about dividing shapes and numbers into equal size pieces called fractions.

Useful information

a $\frac{1}{2}$ means share into 2 equal parts

$\frac{1}{3}$ means share into 3 equal parts

$\frac{1}{4}$ means share into 4 equal parts

b $\frac{2}{3}$ means share into 3 equal parts and have 2 of those parts

$\frac{3}{5}$ means share into 5 equal parts and have 3 of those parts

c $\frac{1}{3}$ of $12 = 12 \div 3 = 4$

$\frac{1}{4}$ of $20 = 20 \div 4 = 5$

$\frac{2}{3}$ of 12: find $\frac{1}{3}$ first ($12 \div 3 = 4$), then $4 \times 2 = 8$

$\frac{3}{4}$ of 20: find $\frac{1}{4}$ first ($20 \div 4 = 5$), then $5 \times 3 = 12$

Number Crunching 2

3 Number Crunching 3

4 Number Crunching 4

Ch 29 Percentages

Ch 29 Percentages

EXTENSION: E5, E6

Drawing Fractions

A Draw and colour $\frac{1}{2}$ of each shape.

Example

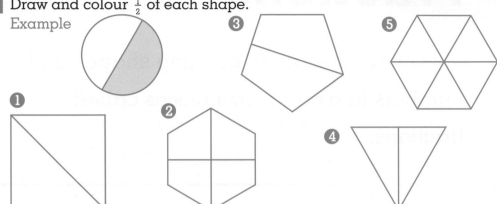

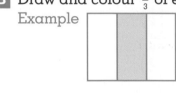

B Draw and colour $\frac{1}{3}$ of each shape.

Example

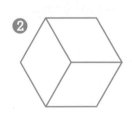

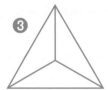

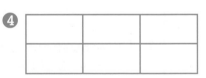

C Draw and colour $\frac{2}{3}$ of each shape.

Example

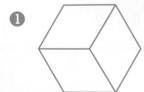

D Draw each shape and colour the fraction named.

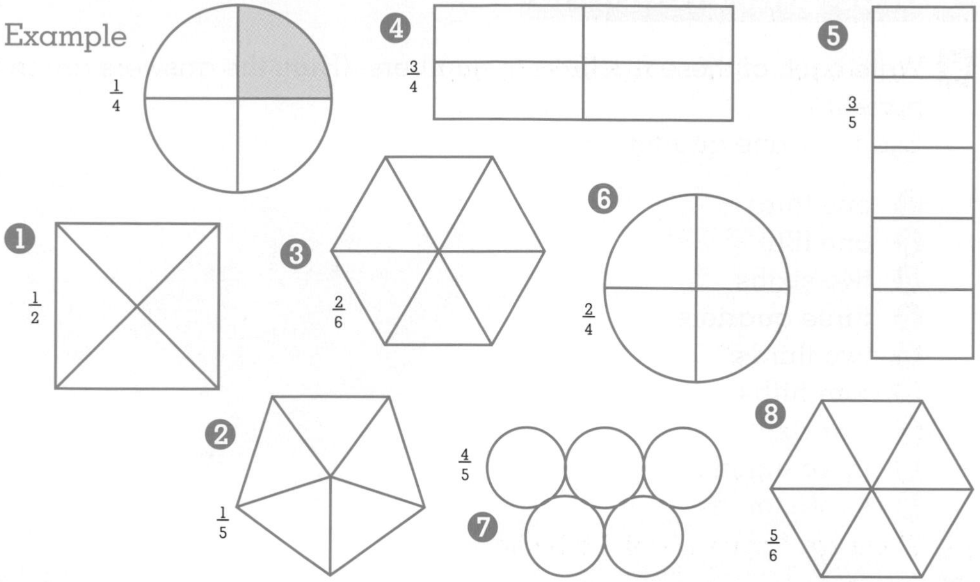

Example
$\frac{1}{4}$

4 $\frac{3}{4}$

5 $\frac{3}{5}$

1 $\frac{1}{2}$

3 $\frac{2}{6}$

6 $\frac{2}{4}$

2 $\frac{1}{5}$

7 $\frac{4}{5}$

8 $\frac{5}{6}$

E What fraction of each of these shapes is shaded?

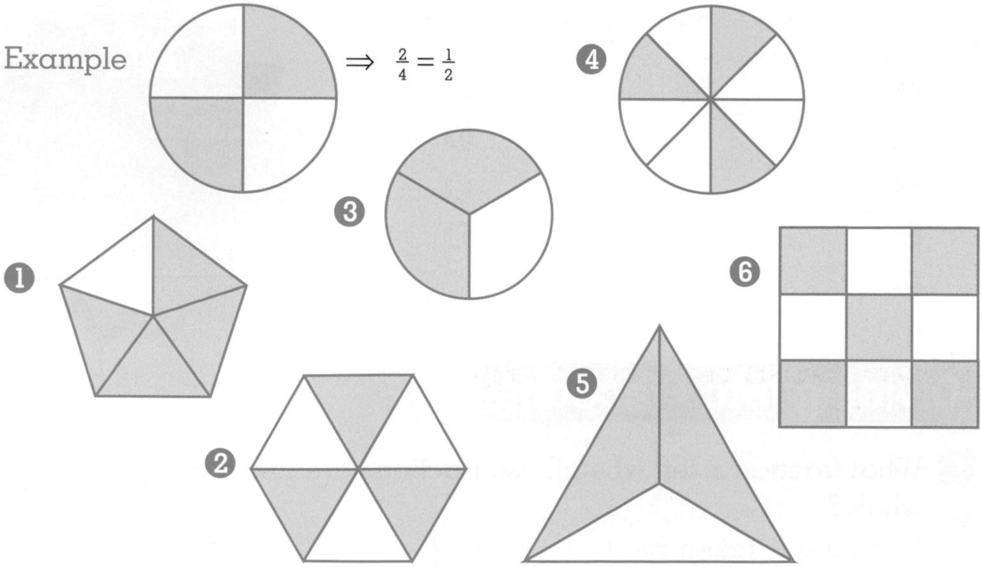

Example $\Rightarrow \frac{2}{4} = \frac{1}{2}$

4

3

1

2

5

6

F Draw shapes which show each of these fractions.

1 $\frac{4}{6}$

2 $\frac{2}{5}$

3 $\frac{1}{7}$

4 $\frac{3}{5}$

5 $\frac{2}{4}$

6 $\frac{1}{10}$

Words and Fractions

G Write each of these fractions in numbers. (Hint: the answers are in the panel.)

Example one quarter $\Rightarrow \frac{1}{4}$

1 one third
2 one fifth
3 two sixths
4 three quarters
5 two thirds
6 four fifths
7 five sixths
8 three eighths
9 seven tenths

H Write each of these fractions as words. (Hint: the words are in the panel.)

Example $\frac{2}{4} \Rightarrow$ two quarters

1 $\frac{3}{5}$ 6 $\frac{4}{6}$

2 $\frac{1}{6}$ 7 $\frac{3}{10}$

3 $\frac{1}{8}$ 8 $\frac{5}{10}$

4 $\frac{1}{2}$ 9 $\frac{2}{5}$

5 $\frac{7}{8}$

quarter

fifth   third

eighth

tenth   half

sixth

Dividing into Fractions

I What fraction is left when these fractions are taken away from the whole?

Example $\frac{1}{2}$ taken $\Rightarrow 1 - \frac{1}{2} = \frac{2}{2} - \frac{1}{2} = \frac{1}{2}$

1 $\frac{1}{3}$ taken   5 $\frac{2}{5}$ taken

2 $\frac{2}{3}$ taken   6 $\frac{3}{8}$ taken

3 $\frac{1}{4}$ taken   7 $\frac{7}{10}$ taken

4 $\frac{1}{5}$ taken

J A parcel of sweets is shared between a brother and sister. Copy and complete the table.

	sweets	brother	sister
Example	chocolates	$\frac{1}{2}$	$\frac{1}{2}$
❶	mints		$\frac{2}{3}$
❷	rock	$\frac{1}{4}$	
❸	fudge	$\frac{2}{4}$	
❹	toffees		$\frac{4}{5}$
❺	boiled sweets	$\frac{5}{6}$	
❻	chewing gum	$\frac{7}{10}$	

K Three friends have won money in lots of different events. Copy and complete the table to show how they share the money.

	event	Tom	Anne	Jim
Example	lottery	$\frac{1}{3}$	$\frac{1}{3}$	$\frac{1}{3}$
❶	raffle	$\frac{2}{5}$		$\frac{1}{5}$
❷	lucky dip	$\frac{1}{7}$		$\frac{3}{7}$
❸	pools		$\frac{2}{8}$	$\frac{3}{8}$
❹	horse racing	$\frac{1}{4}$	$\frac{1}{4}$	

Fractions of an Amount

L Use the drawings to help you work out the number problem.

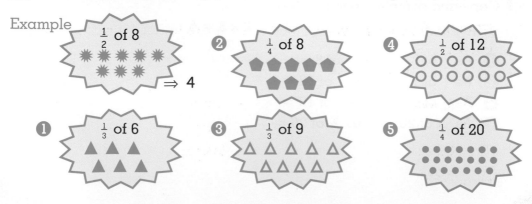

Example: $\frac{1}{2}$ of 8 ⇒ 4

❷ $\frac{1}{4}$ of 8

❹ $\frac{1}{2}$ of 12

❶ $\frac{1}{3}$ of 6

❸ $\frac{1}{3}$ of 9

❺ $\frac{1}{4}$ of 20

M Work out:

Example $\frac{1}{2}$ of 16 = 16 ÷ 2 = 8

1 $\frac{1}{3}$ of 12 =

2 $\frac{1}{4}$ of 16 =

3 $\frac{1}{2}$ of 22 =

4 $\frac{1}{5}$ of 10 =

5 $\frac{1}{3}$ of 21 =

6 $\frac{1}{4}$ of 28 =

7 $\frac{1}{4}$ of 40 =

8 $\frac{1}{5}$ of 25 =

9 $\frac{1}{3}$ of 3 =

N Use the times tables to help you work out the following.

Example $\frac{1}{2}$ of 24 = 24 ÷ 2 = 12

1 $\frac{1}{3}$ of 27 =

2 $\frac{1}{4}$ of 48 =

3 $\frac{1}{5}$ of 45 =

4 $\frac{1}{6}$ of 42 =

5 $\frac{1}{7}$ of 35 =

6 $\frac{1}{8}$ of 48 =

7 $\frac{1}{9}$ of 45 =

8 $\frac{1}{10}$ of 70 =

9 $\frac{1}{11}$ of 22 =

O Use a calculator to work out:

Example $\frac{1}{4}$ of 172 = 172 ÷ 4 = 43

1 $\frac{1}{6}$ of 354 =

2 $\frac{1}{8}$ of 784 =

3 $\frac{1}{3}$ of 942 =

4 $\frac{1}{7}$ of 497 =

5 $\frac{1}{10}$ of 930 =

6 $\frac{1}{10}$ of 2410 =

P Copy and complete each of these.

Example As $\frac{1}{3}$ of 9 = 3, so $\frac{2}{3}$ of 9 = 2 × 3 = 6

1 As $\frac{1}{4}$ of 8 = 2, so $\frac{3}{4}$ of 8 =

2 As $\frac{1}{4}$ of 12 = 3, so $\frac{3}{4}$ of 12 =

3 As $\frac{1}{5}$ of 10 = 2, so $\frac{2}{5}$ of 10 =

4 As $\frac{1}{10}$ of 20 = 2, so $\frac{3}{10}$ of 20 =

Q By first working out $\frac{1}{3}$, find:

Example $\frac{1}{3}$ of 6 = 6 ÷ 3 = 2, $\frac{2}{3}$ of 6 = 2 × 2 = 4

1 $\frac{2}{3}$ of 12 =   **4** $\frac{2}{3}$ of 30 =

2 $\frac{2}{3}$ of 15 =   **5** $\frac{2}{3}$ of 3 =

3 $\frac{2}{3}$ of 27 =

R By first working out $\frac{1}{4}$, find:

Example $\frac{1}{4}$ of 12 = 12 ÷ 4 = 3, $\frac{3}{4}$ of 12 = 3 × 3 = 9

1 $\frac{3}{4}$ of 20 =   **4** $\frac{2}{4}$ of 28 =

2 $\frac{2}{4}$ of 40 =   **5** $\frac{3}{4}$ of 32 =

3 $\frac{3}{4}$ of 4 =

S Work out:

Example $\frac{2}{3}$ of £21 = 21 ÷ 3 × 2 = £14

1 $\frac{3}{4}$ of 16 kg =   **4** $\frac{3}{5}$ of 50 litres =

2 $\frac{2}{5}$ of 40 cm =   **5** $\frac{2}{7}$ of 49 mins =

3 $\frac{4}{5}$ of 25 m =   **6** $\frac{7}{10}$ of £90 =

T Use a calculator to work out:

1 $\frac{2}{3}$ of 765   **5** $\frac{3}{10}$ of 760

2 $\frac{3}{4}$ of 568   **6** $\frac{5}{7}$ of 518

3 $\frac{2}{5}$ of 425   **7** $\frac{4}{5}$ of 1315

4 $\frac{3}{8}$ of 464   **8** $\frac{8}{9}$ of 828

U Copy and complete the table to find $\frac{1}{2}$ and $\frac{1}{4}$ of each of these amounts of money.

	money	halved ($\frac{1}{2}$)	quartered ($\frac{1}{4}$)
Example	20p	20 ÷ 2 = 10p	20 ÷ 4 = 5p
1	12p		
2	16p		
3	28p		
4	40p		
5	48p		
6	72p		
7	80p		
8	56p		
9	64p		
10	92p		

V Copy and complete the table to find $\frac{1}{2}$ and $\frac{1}{4}$ of each of these amounts of money.

	money	halved ($\frac{1}{2}$)	quartered ($\frac{1}{4}$)
Example	£1.20	120 ÷ 2 = 60p	120 ÷ 4 = 30p
1	£1.60		
2	£1.00		
3	£2.00		
4	£6.00		
5	£3.60		
6	£10.40		
7	£1.16		
8	£1.52		
9	£1.96		
10	£2.28		

W Look at the pictures to help you to work out these questions.

Example

 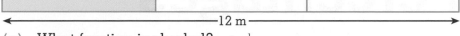

(a) What fraction is shaded? $\Rightarrow \frac{1}{3}$
(b) How long is the shaded part? $\Rightarrow \frac{1}{3}$ of $12 = 12 \div 3 = 4$ m

❶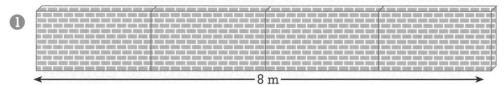

(a) What fraction of the wall is shaded?
(b) How long is the shaded part?
(c) How long is the unshaded part?

❷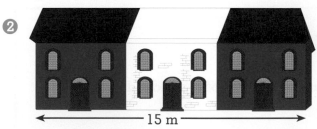

(a) What fraction of the houses is shaded?
(b) How long is the shaded part?

❸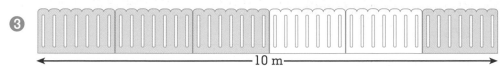

(a) What fraction of the fence is shaded?
(b) How long is the shaded part?

❹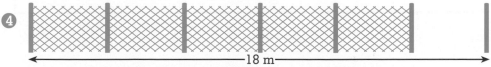

(a) What fraction of the fence has been put up?
(b) How long is the fence so far?

✓ **Checking your answers** ? **Testing how much you know**

Percentages

This chapter is about using simple percentages (25%, 50% and 75%) to find out the percentage of an amount, and to convert percentages to and from fractions.

Useful information

a percentage means an amount out of a hundred
so 10% means 10 out of 100

b the sign for percentage is %

c percentages and fractions

$25\% = \frac{25}{100} = \frac{1}{4}$

$50\% = \frac{50}{100} = \frac{1}{2}$

$75\% = \frac{75}{100} = \frac{3}{4}$

Ch 28 Fractions

Ch 28 Fractions

EXTENSION: E4

Fractions and Percentages

A Choose an answer from the bubble to describe the percentage left of each item.

Example $\frac{1}{2}$ full $\Rightarrow$ $\frac{1}{2}$ empty = 50%

25%   50%   0%   75%   100%

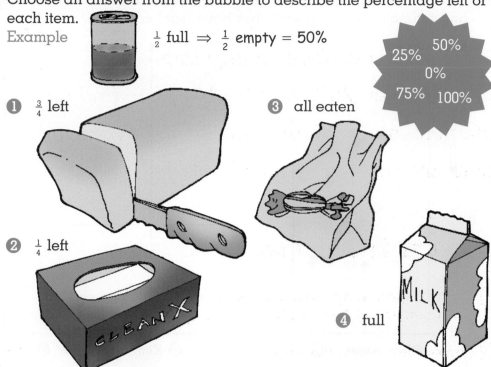

❶ $\frac{3}{4}$ left

❷ $\frac{1}{4}$ left

❸   all eaten

❹   full

B Choose a fraction from the bubble to describe these test marks.

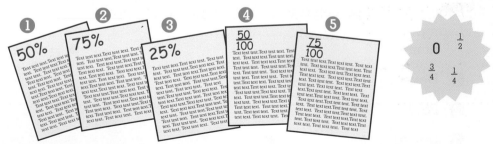

❶ 50%

❷ 75%

❸ 25%

❹ $\frac{50}{100}$

❺ $\frac{75}{100}$

0   $\frac{1}{2}$ $\frac{3}{4}$ $\frac{1}{4}$

C Copy and complete.

Example $\frac{1}{2}$ marks $\Rightarrow$ 50%

❶   75% = $\frac{?}{?}$

❷ $\frac{25}{100}$ = ___ %

❸   full marks $\Rightarrow$ ___ %

❹ $\frac{75}{100}$ = ___ %

❺ $\frac{20}{20}$ = ___ %

❻ $\frac{0}{15}$ = ___ %

❼ $\frac{20}{40}$ = ___ %

Estimating Percentages

D In a charity event each pupil is trying to raise £10. Look at the chart and estimate the percentage they have reached.

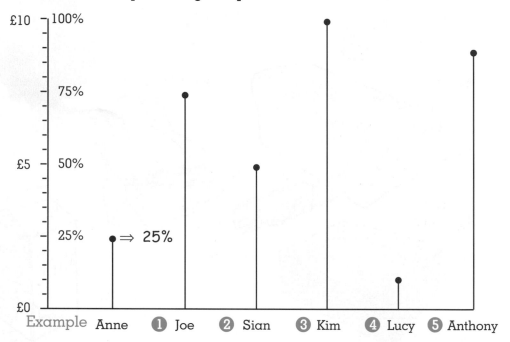

E The record throw of the shot-put in the school is 10 metres.
Estimate what percentage of that length these pupils have thrown.

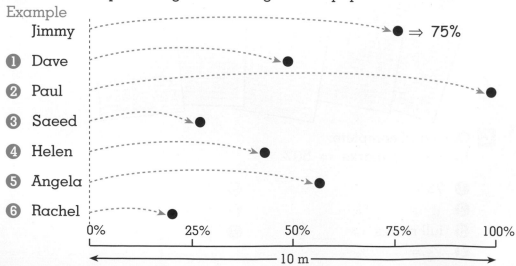

Working Out Percentages

F Find 50% of:
Example £4 $\Rightarrow$ $\frac{1}{2}$ of 4 = £2

1. 20 seconds
2. 12 m
3. 22 kg
4. 50 litres
5. 40 seconds

6. 18 cm
7. 5 tonnes
8. 36p
9. 26 mm

G Find 25% of:
Example £100 $\Rightarrow$ $\frac{1}{4}$ of 100 = £25

1. 12 kg
2. 200 litres
3. 4 km
4. 20 minutes
5. £10

6. 1000 kg
7. 40 cm
8. 48 hours
9. £2

H Find 75% of:
Example 4 kg $\Rightarrow$ $\frac{3}{4}$ of 4 = 3 kg

1. 20 seconds
2. 100 years
3. £40

4. 2 days
5. 12 mm

I If each child has a 50% rise in their pocket-money, copy and complete the table.

	name	old pocket-money	rise in pocket-money	new pocket-money
Example	Ian	£2	£1	£2 + £1 = £3
1	Colin	£4		
2	James	£10		
3	Andrew	£6		
4	Samantha	£8		
5	Joanna	£5		
6	Becky	£1		
7	Emma	£15		

J Each of the chocolate bars has 25% extra free. Copy and complete the table.

	name	weight of old bar	extra 25%	weight of new bar
Example	Snacker	100 g	25 g	100 + 25 = 125 g
1	Venus bar	80 g		
2	Silky bar	200 g		
3	Brix bite	160 g		
4	Crumblie	400 g		
5	Trekker	320 g		
6	Stars bar	40 g		
7	Tiger bar	60 g		

K Work out these questions.

Example John has £10, and is given 50% more. How much does he now have?   50% of £10 = £5   Total ⇒ £10 + £5 = £15

❶ Linda has £10 and spends 50%. How much does she have left?
❷ George has 12 squares of chocolate and he eats 25% of them. How many squares does he have left?
❸ Jane has £100 in the bank, but she spends 75% of it.
   (a)   How much money does she spend?
   (b)   How much money does she have left?

❹ Danny buys 50 sweets and gives 50% away. How many sweets does he have left?
❺ Kelly is given a 25% pay rise. If she used to earn £40, how much does she earn now?

Percentage Scales

L In each of these questions find the percentage of flour, milk, margarine and sugar in each recipe.

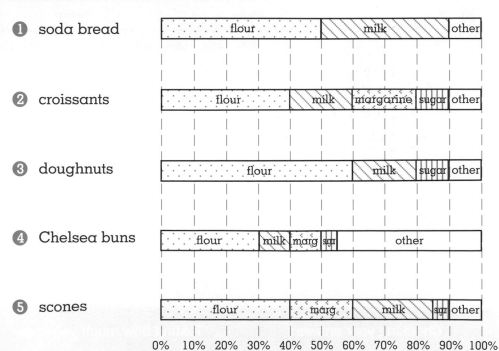

❶ soda bread

❷ croissants

❸ doughnuts

❹ Chelsea buns

❺ scones

0%   10%   20%   30%   40%   50%   60%   70%   80%   90%   100%

M The chart shows how marks are given in an examination. Write down the percentage marks for the different parts.

Example

English – Writing ⇒ 40%   Spelling ⇒ 30%   Speaking ⇒ 30%

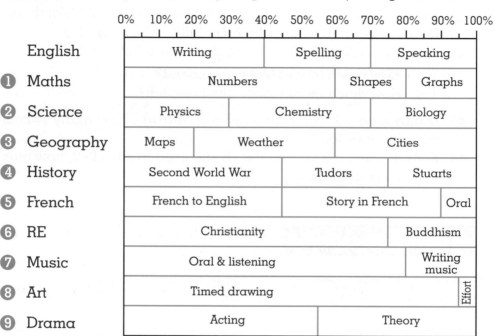

| | 0% | 10% | 20% | 30% | 40% | 50% | 60% | 70% | 80% | 90% | 100% |

English: Writing | Spelling | Speaking

1 Maths: Numbers | Shapes | Graphs

2 Science: Physics | Chemistry | Biology

3 Geography: Maps | Weather | Cities

4 History: Second World War | Tudors | Stuarts

5 French: French to English | Story in French | Oral

6 RE: Christianity | Buddhism

7 Music: Oral & listening | Writing music

8 Art: Timed drawing | Effort

9 Drama: Acting | Theory

| 0% | 10% | 20% | 30% | 40% | 50% | 60% | 70% | 80% | 90% | 100% |

Finding Rules

This chapter is about finding rules and patterns in shapes and numbers.

A calculator is used when needed.

Useful information

a look carefully at the diagrams, and draw the next ones if you want more help to complete the tables

b a rule tells you how to make a new group of numbers from your starting numbers

e.g. starting number → $\boxed{+\,5}$ → new number

this rule adds 5 to all its starting numbers, so you can make a table like this:

starting number	new number
1	6
2	7
3	8
4	9
etc.	etc.

you can use this rule to predict what comes next

c use a calculator display turned upside down to make letters and words

e.g. **7 becomes L upside down**

Ch 5 Patterns
18 Number Machines

1 Backwards Calculations
Ch 32 Formulas

Patterns

A Draw these diagrams, and the next two in the pattern. Copy and complete the table. Find the rule.

Example ① ②

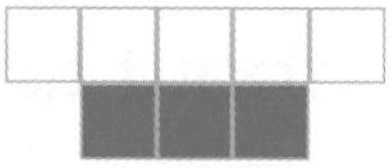

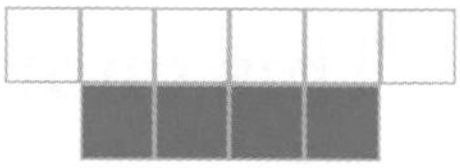

	number of black squares	number of white squares
Example	2	4
①	3	
②	4	
③	5	
④	6	
⑤	7	
⑥	8	

Rule is:

number of black squares → ☐ → number of white squares

B Draw these diagrams, and the next one. Copy and complete the table. Find the rule.

Example ① ②

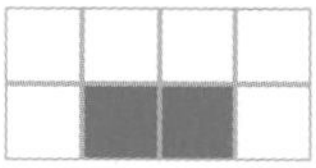

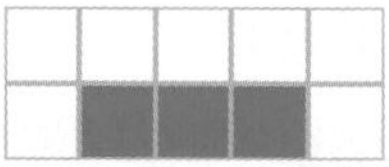

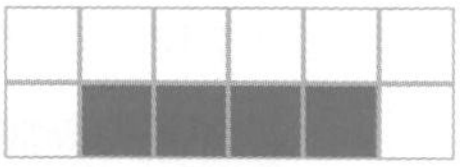

	number of black squares	number of white squares
Example	2	6
①	3	
②	4	
③	5	
④	6	
⑤	7	
⑥	8	
⑦	9	

Rule is:

number of black squares → ☐ → number of white squares

C Draw these diagrams, and the next one. Copy and complete the table. Find the rule.

Example   ❶

	number of black squares	number of white squares
Example	6	2
❶	7	
❷	8	
❸	10	
❹	5	
❺	9	
❻	12	

Rule is:

number of black squares → ▢ → number of white squares

D Draw these diagrams and the next one. Copy and complete the table. Find the rule.

Example   ❶   ❷

	number of black squares	number of white squares
Example	3	6
❶	4	
❷	5	
❸	6	
❹	2	
❺	10	
❻	15	

Rule is:

number of black squares → ▢ → number of white squares

E Draw these diagrams and the next one. Copy and complete the table
Find the rule.

Example   ①   ②

	number of black squares	number of white squares
Example	2	8
①	3	
②	4	
③	5	
④	6	
⑤	1	
⑥	8	

Rule is:

number of black squares → ☐ → number of white squares

F Draw these diagrams. Copy and complete the table. Find the rule.

Example   ①   ②

	number of black squares	number of white squares
Example	2	7
①	3	
②	4	
③	5	
④	6	
⑤	7	
⑥	8	
⑦	9	

Rule is:

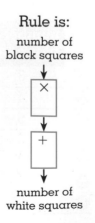

number of black squares

↓

×

↓

+

↓

number of white squares

G Draw these diagrams. Copy and complete the table. Find the rule.

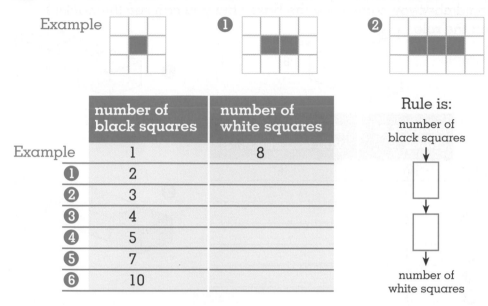

Example   **①**   **②**

	number of black squares	number of white squares
Example	1	8
①	2	
②	3	
③	4	
④	5	
⑤	7	
⑥	10	

Rule is:

number of
black squares

↓

☐

↓

☐

↓

number of
white squares

H The drawings show piles of cubes. Work out the number of faces of the cubes that can be seen. (You cannot see the base but remember the faces on the back of the cube.) Find the rule.

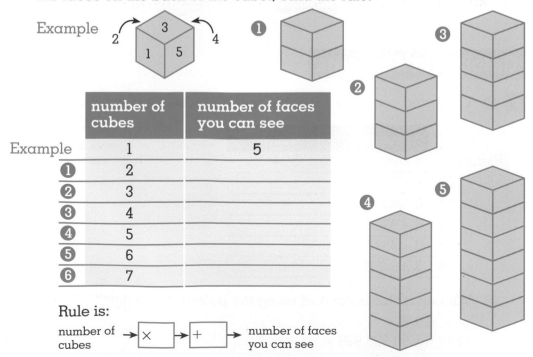

	number of cubes	number of faces you can see
Example	1	5
①	2	
②	3	
③	4	
④	5	
⑤	6	
⑥	7	

Rule is:

number of
cubes → ☐ × → ☐ + → number of faces
you can see

223

I The drawings show rows of cubes. Copy and complete the table. (Remember you cannot see the bases but you can see the backs.) Find the rule.

Example

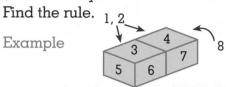

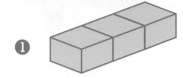

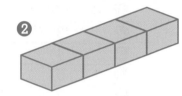

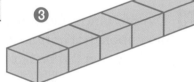

	number of cubes	number of faces you can see
Example	2	8
①	3	
②	4	
③	5	
④	6	
⑤	7	
⑥	8	
⑦	10	

Rule is:

number of cubes number of faces you can see

Calculator Patterns

J ① Copy and complete this table and describe the pattern you see.

	calculation	answer
Example	6×99	594
ⓐ	6×999	
ⓑ	6×9999	
ⓒ	$6 \times 99\,999$	
ⓓ	$6 \times 999\,999$	
ⓔ	$6 \times 9\,999\,999$	

② Without a calculator and using the pattern, work out:

(a) $6 \times 9 =$

(b) $6 \times 99\,999\,999 =$

K **①** Copy and complete this table.

	calculation	answer
Example	3×37	111
ⓐ	6×37	
ⓑ	9×37	
ⓒ	12×37	
ⓓ	15×37	

② Describe the pattern in the answers.

③ Without a calculator and using the pattern, work out:

(a) $18 \times 37 =$

(b) $27 \times 37 =$

L **①** Copy and complete this table.

	calculation	answer
Example	11×11	121
ⓐ	11×12	
ⓑ	11×13	
ⓒ	11×14	
ⓓ	11×15	

② Describe the pattern in the answers.

③ Without a calculator and using the pattern, work out:

(a) $11 \times 16 =$

(b) $11 \times 17 =$

(c) $11 \times 18 =$

M **1** Copy and complete this table.

	calculation	answer
Example	9×99	891
ⓐ	8×99	
ⓑ	7×99	
ⓒ	6×99	
ⓓ	5×99	

2 Describe the pattern in the answers.

3 Without a calculator and using the pattern, work out:

(a) $4 \times 99 =$

(b) $3 \times 99 =$

(c) $2 \times 99 =$

N **1** Copy and complete this table.

	calculation	answer
Example	$7 \times 15\ 873$	111 111
ⓐ	$14 \times 15\ 873$	
ⓑ	$21 \times 15\ 873$	
ⓒ	$28 \times 15\ 873$	
ⓓ	$35 \times 15\ 873$	
ⓔ	$42 \times 15\ 873$	
ⓕ	$49 \times 15\ 873$	

2 Describe the pattern in the answers.

3 Without a calculator and using the pattern, work out:

(a) $56 \times 15\ 873 =$

(b) $63 \times 15\ 873 =$

④ Now continue this table showing the pattern continuing.

	calculation	answer
Example	70 × 15 873	1 111 110
ⓐ	77 × 15 873	
ⓑ	84 × 15 873	
ⓒ	91 × 15 873	
ⓓ	98 × 15 873	

⑤ Describe the pattern in the answers.

⑥ Without a calculator and using the pattern, work out:
   (a) 119 × 15 873 =
   (b) 126 × 15 873 =

[0] When you turn a calculator display upside down, some of the numbers look like letters.

① Use a calculator to complete this table.

number	letter
0	O
1	I
2	Z
3	
4	
5	
6	
7	
8	
9	

2   Try these sums on a calculator and turn the answers upside down to give a word.

Example $154\,690 \div 2 = 77345 = ShELL$

(a) $2191 - 1458 =$

(b) $132\,925 \div 25 =$

(c) $53\,045 \times 3 \div 3 =$

(d) $3867 \times 2 =$

3   Make up some words using the letters from **0 1**, turn it into a number and make up a sum to fit.

	word	number	sum
Example	OIL	710	720 – 10
a			
b			
c			
d			
e			

✓ Checking your answers   **Testing how much you know**

Backwards Calculations

This chapter is about reversing calculations and using the opposite sign to solve number problems.

Useful information

a opposites
+ and –

× and ÷

b to solve problems

? → +5 → 20   becomes   20 → –5 → ?

? → –7 → 14   becomes   14 → +7 → ?

? → ÷ 3 → 15   becomes   15 → × 3 → ?

? → × 2 → 10   becomes   10 → ÷ 2 → ?

c for longer problems on a calculator always press = after each stage

? × 2, then + 5 = 25 in reverse becomes 25 – 5 = 20, then 20 ÷ 2 = 10

3 Number Crunching 2

3 Number Crunching 3

4 Number Crunching 4

18 Number Machines

Ch 32 Formulas

Single Calculations

A By doing the working in reverse, find the missing number.

Example $? \rightarrow \boxed{+ 5} \rightarrow 10 \Rightarrow 10 - 5 = 5$

1 $? \rightarrow \boxed{- 2} \rightarrow 12$ **5** $? \rightarrow \boxed{- 9} \rightarrow 18$

2 $? \rightarrow \boxed{+ 7} \rightarrow 15$ **6** $? \rightarrow \boxed{- 23} \rightarrow 4$

3 $? \rightarrow \boxed{- 10} \rightarrow 5$ **7** $? \rightarrow \boxed{+ 32} \rightarrow 50$

4 $? \rightarrow \boxed{+ 12} \rightarrow 17$ **8** $? \rightarrow \boxed{- 26} \rightarrow 26$

B Use your calculator to help solve these calculations, by working in reverse.

Example $? \rightarrow \boxed{+ 76} \rightarrow 150 \Rightarrow 150 - 76 = 74$

1 $? \rightarrow \boxed{- 420} \rightarrow 132$ **5** $? \rightarrow \boxed{+ 191} \rightarrow 706$

2 $? \rightarrow \boxed{+ 302} \rightarrow 400$ **6** $? \rightarrow \boxed{- 897} \rightarrow 82$

3 $? \rightarrow \boxed{- 156} \rightarrow 47$ **7** $? \rightarrow \boxed{+ 1193} \rightarrow 2000$

4 $? \rightarrow \boxed{+ 299} \rightarrow 501$ **8** $? \rightarrow \boxed{- 1193} \rightarrow 2000$

C By doing the working in reverse, find the missing number.

Example $? \rightarrow \boxed{\times 2} \rightarrow 10 \Rightarrow 10 \div 2 = 5$

1 $? \rightarrow \boxed{\div 2} \rightarrow 6$ **5** $? \rightarrow \boxed{\times 5} \rightarrow 55$

2 $? \rightarrow \boxed{\times 3} \rightarrow 18$ **6** $? \rightarrow \boxed{\div 5} \rightarrow 7$

3 $? \rightarrow \boxed{\div 3} \rightarrow 5$ **7** $? \rightarrow \boxed{\times 10} \rightarrow 80$

4 $? \rightarrow \boxed{\times 4} \rightarrow 32$ **8** $? \rightarrow \boxed{\div 10} \rightarrow 4$

D Use a calculator to help you work out the value of the missing number.

Example ? → $\boxed{\times 15}$ → 375 ⇒ 375 ÷ 15 = 25

1. ? → $\boxed{\div 8}$ → 37
2. ? → $\boxed{\times 17}$ → 408
3. ? → $\boxed{\div 7}$ → 101
4. ? → $\boxed{\times 42}$ → 1176
5. ? → $\boxed{\times 25}$ → 1250
6. ? → $\boxed{\div 123}$ → 16
7. ? → $\boxed{\times 39}$ → 1716
8. ? → $\boxed{\div 239}$ → 116

E Work out these questions using a number machine and then find the missing number.

Example I think of a number and add 42. The answer is 57.
What number did I think of? ⇒ ? → $\boxed{+ 42}$ → 57 ⇒ 57 − 42 = 15

1. I think of a number and take away 16. The answer is 15.
   What number did I think of?
2. I think of a number and divide by 3. The answer is 7.
   What number did I think of?

Double Calculations

F Work backwards to find the missing number.

Example ? → +3 → −5 → 6 ⇒ 6 + 5 − 3 = 8

1. ? → −4 → +8 → 11
2. ? → −2 → −5 → 3
3. ? → +11 → +14 → 30
4. ? → −26 → +3 → 15
5. ? → +37 → −50 → 12
6. ? → −47 → +31 → 43
7. ? → +63 → −20 → 97
8. ? → −101 → +49 → 150
9. ? → +39 → +48 → 103

G Use a calculator when you need it to find the value of the missing number.

Example ? $\times 2$ $+ 3$ → 11 ⟹ $(11 - 3) \div 2 = 4$

1 ? $- 3$ $\times 3$ → 9

2 ? $+ 4$ $\times 2$ → 24

3 ? $- 7$ $\times 3$ → 24

4 ? $+ 15$ $\times 4$ → 80

5 ? $- 21$ $\times 5$ → 20

6 ? $\times 6$ $+ 7$ → 19

7 ? $\times 9$ $- 29$ → 7

8 ? $\times 7$ $+ 1$ → 50

9 ? $- 17$ $\times 3$ → 99

H Find the missing number by working backwards.

Example ? → $+ 3$ → $\div 2$ → 6 ⟹ $6 \times 2 - 3 = 9$

1 ? → $\div 3$ → $- 3$ → 1   **5** ? → $+ 17$ → $\div 4$ → 15

2 ? → $+ 7$ → $\div 4$ → 4   **6** ? → $- 31$ → $\div 5$ → 6

3 ? → $\times 2$ → $\div 3$ → 4   **7** ? → $\div 7$ → $- 12$ → 0

4 ? → $\div 5$ → $\times 2$ → 18   **8** ? → $\div 3$ → $\div 5$ → 1

I Solve these problems by reversing the signs.

Example ? × 2, then + 7 = 17 ⇒ 17 − 7, then ÷ 2 = 5

1 ? − 10, then + 11 = 22   **6** ? ÷ 4, then − 15 = 0
2 ? + 7, then × 2 = 28   **7** ? + 19, then × 2 = 76
3 ? − 12, then × 3 = 24   **8** ? − 47, then × 4 = 52
4 ? ÷ 6, then + 15 = 20   **9** ? − 91, then × 7 = 49
5 ? × 3, then + 14 = 50

J Find the number in each question.

Example

I think of a number, add 3 and divide the result by 2. The answer is 5.

? → | + 3 | → | ÷ 2 | → 5

becomes 5 × 2 = 10, then − 3 = 7 So ? is 7

1 I think of a number, take away 5 and multiply the result by 3. The answer is 15.

2 I think of a number, multiply it by 2 and add 7 to the result. The answer is 19.

3 I think of a number, divide it by 2 and take 7 away from the result. The answer is 3.

4 I think of a number, multiply it by 3 and take away 3 from the result. The answer is 24.

5 I think of a number, take away 3 and divide the result by 2. The answer is 8.

6 I think of a number, divide it by 5 and multiply the result by 3. The answer is 12.

Checking your answers   **Testing how much you know**

Formulas

This chapter is about rules given in words (or numbers) for solving problems. It includes some rules that are used in real-life situations.

Useful information

short formulas

this is a formula to work out the price for different size bouquets of flowers:

number of flowers $\rightarrow$ $\boxed{\times 2}$ $\rightarrow$ $\boxed{+1}$ $\rightarrow$ price in £

you can also use letters to stand for the amounts in the question to make it quicker to write down

here, n stands for number of flowers,
     p stands for price in £

 $\rightarrow n \times 2 + 1 = p$

to find out the price of 10 flowers, put 10 instead of n in the formula

$10 \times 2 + 1 = p$

$21 = p$

so price $\rightarrow$ £21

Ch 3 Number Crunching
Ch 13 Number Crunching
Ch 14 Number Crunching
Ch 15 Decimals 1
Ch 18 Number Machines
Ch 23 Decimals 2
Ch 30 Finding Rules

Ch 34 Filling Space

Single Formulas

A This is the formula to change inches into centimetres:

number of inches → $\boxed{\times 2.54}$ → number of centimetres (cm)

Change these inches into centimetres.
Example 4 inches = ___ cm ⟹ 4 × 2.54 = 10.16 cm

1. 3 inches = ___ cm
2. 5 inches = ___ cm
3. 8 inches = ___ cm
4. 10 inches = ___ cm
5. 12 inches = ___ cm

B Use the formula in reverse to change these centimetres into inches.
Example 10 cm = ___ inches ⟹ 10 ÷ 2.54 = 3.93 inches

1. 22 cm = ___ inches
2. 22.86 cm = ___ inches
3. 45 cm = ___ inches
4. 100 cm = ___ inches

C This is the formula to change pounds weight into kilograms:

number of pounds (lb) → $\boxed{\div\ 2.2}$ → number of kilograms (kg)

Change these pounds into kilograms.
Example 4 lb = ___ kg ⟹ 4 ÷ 2.2 = 1.81 kg

1. 10 lb = ___ kg
2. 4.4 lb = ___ kg
3. 15 lb = ___ kg
4. 33 lb = ___ kg

By working in reverse change these kilograms into pounds.

5. ___ lb = 6 kg
6. ___ lb = 45 kg

D This is the formula to change pints into litres:

number of pints → $\div 1.76$ → number of litres

Change these pints into litres.
Example 2 pints = ___ litres ⟹ 2 ÷ 1.76 = 1.13 litres

1 1 pint = ___ litres
2 1.76 pints = ___ litres
3 8.8 pints = ___ litres

By working in reverse, change the litres to pints.

4 ___ pints = 4 litres
5 ___ pints = 10 litres
6 ___ pints = 2 litres

E This is the formula to change miles into kilometres (km):

number of miles → $\times 1.6$ → number of kilometres

Change these miles into kilometres.
Example 1 mile = ___ km ⟹ 1 × 1.6 = 1.6 km

1 3 miles = ___ km
2 5 miles = ___ km
3 62.5 miles = ___ km
4 100 miles = ___ km

By working in reverse, change these kilometres to miles.

5 ___ miles = 16 km
6 ___ miles = 40 km
7 ___ miles = 320 km
8 ___ miles = 1 000 km

Two-part Formulas

These are the formulas that a photo company uses to work out the price for different size prints:

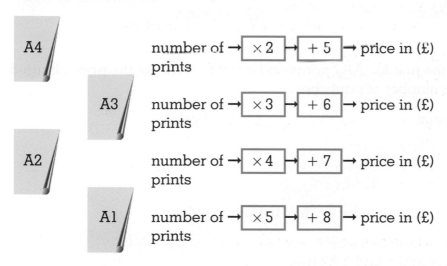

number of → ×2 → +5 → price in (£)
prints

number of → ×3 → +6 → price in (£)
prints

number of → ×4 → +7 → price in (£)
prints

number of → ×5 → +8 → price in (£)
prints

F Copy the rule for A4 prints and use it to work out the price charged for the number of prints below.
Example 1 print ⟹ 1 × 2 + 5 = £7

1. 2 prints
2. 4 prints
3. 7 prints
4. 10 prints
5. 14 prints

G Copy the rule for A3 prints and use it to work out the price charged for the number of prints below.

1. 1 print
2. 3 prints
3. 5 prints
4. 9 prints
5. 10 prints
6. 17 prints

237

H Copy the rule for A2 prints and use it to work out the price charged for the number of prints below.

① 1 print
② 2 prints
③ 6 prints

④ 9 prints
⑤ 10 prints
⑥ 13 prints

I Copy the rule for A1 prints and use it to work out the price charged for the number of prints below.

① 1 print
② 3 prints
③ 4 prints

④ 5 prints
⑤ 8 prints
⑥ 10 prints

J Work out the price for each of the prints below.

① 1 print of each size
② 2 A4 prints and 2 A2 prints
③ 2 prints of each size
④ 100 A4 prints
⑤ 10 prints of each size

K This is the formula to change degrees Fahrenheit (°F) into degrees Celsius (°C):

number of degrees Fahrenheit (°F) → -32 → $\times 0.55$ → number of degrees Celsius (°C)

Change from Fahrenheit to Celsius:
Example $50\ °F =$ ___ $°C \Rightarrow (50 - 32) \times 0.55 = 9.9\ °C$

① $60\ °F =$ ___ $°C$
② $32\ °F =$ ___ $°C$
③ $42\ °F =$ ___ $°C$

By working in reverse, change these temperatures from Celsius to Fahrenheit.

④ ___ $°F = 27.5\ °C$
⑤ ___ $°F = 22\ °C$

Number Formulas

L Change these formulas into a letter form, where *n* is the number of prints and *p* is the price in pounds (£).

Example number of prints (*n*) → $\times 2$ — $+5$ → price (*p*) becomes $n \times 2 + 5 = p$

❶ number of prints (*n*) → $\times 3$ — $+2$ → price (*p*) becomes _____

❷ number of prints (*n*) → $\times 2$ — $+8$ → price (*p*) becomes _____

❸ number of prints (*n*) → $\div 3$ — -7 → price (*p*) becomes _____

❹ number of prints (*n*) → $\times 5$ — -4 → price (*p*) becomes _____

❺ number of prints (*n*) → $\div 2$ — $+6$ → price (*p*) becomes _____

M Use these formulas to calculate the time taken to cook chickens:

$$w \times 15 + 20 = t \qquad\qquad w \times 30 + 20 = t$$

w is weight in pounds   w is weight in kilograms
t is time in minutes   t is time in minutes

Copy and complete this table working out the time taken to cook chickens of various weights and the time cooking started if all the chickens are ready to eat at 6 pm.

	weight	time taken to cook	time cooking started
Example	2 lb	$2 \times 15 + 20 = 50$	6 pm – 50 min = 5.10 pm
①	3 lb		
②	1 kg		
③	4 lb		
④	4 kg		
⑤	5 lb		
⑥	2 kg		
⑦	6 lb		
⑧	9 lb		
⑨	3 kg		
⑩	5 kg		

Use these rules for working out different bills to answer **N** , **O** and **P** .

Electricity	$p = n \times 0.13 + 18$
Gas	$p = n \times 0.09 + 12$
Water	$p = n \times 0.04 + 8$

p = price (£)
n = number of units

N Copy the formula for electricity bills and work out the price.
Example number of units is 70 $\Rightarrow$ $70 \times 0.13 + 18 = £27.10$

① when number of units is 100
② when number of units is 270
③ when $n = 350$
④ when $n = 710$
⑤ when $n = 946$

O Copy the formula for gas bills and work out the price:

1. when number of units = 40
2. when number of units = 90
3. when number of units = 140
4. when $n = 200$
5. when $n = 460$
6. when $n = 690$

P Copy the formula for water bills and find p:

1. when $n = 240$
2. when $n = 300$
3. when $n = 560$
4. when $n = 930$
5. when $n = 1020$
6. when $n = 1763$

Recipes

Q Both of these recipes serve four people:

Mince Pie
8 oz plain flour
4 oz margarine
2 tablespoons water
8 oz mincemeat
1 tablespoon brandy

Tea Cakes
16 oz plain flour
2 teaspoons sugar
4 oz currants
1 oz fresh yeast
8 oz warm milk

1. Write out a recipe for mince pie to serve eight people
2. Write out a recipe for tea cakes to serve twelve people
3. Write out a recipe for mince pie to serve two people
4. How much plain flour is needed to make both recipes?
5. Write out a recipe for mince pie to serve twelve people

✓ **Checking your answers**   ⦿ **Testing how much you know**

Co-ordinates

This chapter is about finding the position of something by using points on a grid. The numbers which give that position are called the co-ordinates and grid references.

Useful information

a labelling points

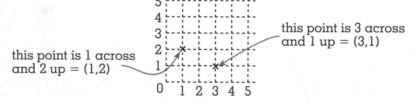

this point is 1 across and 2 up = (1,2)

this point is 3 across and 1 up = (3,1)

always read across and then up

b four-figure grid references

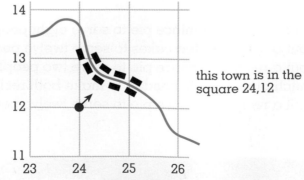

this town is in the square 24,12

the square's contents are defined by the co-ordinates of the bottom left corner of the square

Ch 8 Directions

Reading Co-ordinates

A Look at the map and give the co-ordinates of each of the letters.
Example A is at (4,2)

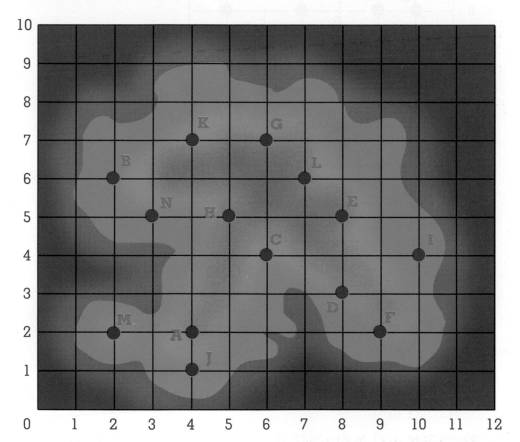

1. B = (___ , ___)
2. C = (___ , ___)
3. D = (___ , ___)
4. E = (___ , ___)
5. F = (___ , ___)
6. G = (___ , ___)
7. H = (___ , ___)

8. I = (___ , ___)
9. J = (___ , ___)
10. K = (___ , ___)
11. L = (___ , ___)
12. M = (___ , ___)
13. N = (___ , ___)

B Use the grid to solve the coded messages.

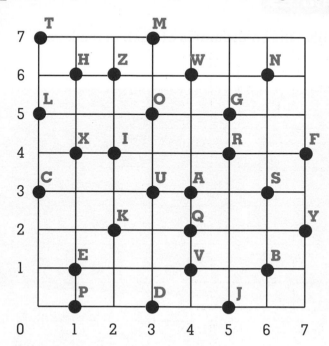

❶ (0,3) (3,5) (3,5) (5,4) (3,0) (2,4) (6,6) (4,3) (0,7) (1,1) 6,3) –

Example   *C*   *O*

     (4,3) (5,4) (1,1) – (1,1) (4,3) (6,3) (7,2)

❷ (5,5) (3,5) – (4,3) (0,3) (5,4) (3,5) (6,3) (6,3) – (0,7) (1,6) (1,1) (6,6) –
(3,3) (1,0)

❸ (3,3) (6,3) (1,1) – (0,7) (1,6) (1,1) – (6,3) (4,2) (3,3) (4,3) (5,4) (1,1) (6,3)
– (4,3) (6,6) (3,0) – (0,5) (2,4) (6,6) (1,1) (6,3)

❹ (4,6) (1,6) (4,3) (0,7) – (4,3) (5,4) (1,1) – (0,7) (1,6) (1,1) –
(0,5) (1,1) (0,7) (0,7) (1,1) (5,4) (6,3) – (3,5) (6,6) – (0,7) (1,6) (1,1) –
(6,1) (3,5) (0,7) (0,7) (3,5) (3,7) – (0,5) (2,4) (6,6) (1,1)

C Find the letters on the grid which have the given co-ordinates.
Example (4,5) is C

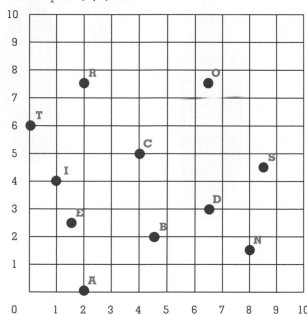

① $(6\frac{1}{2}, 7\frac{1}{2})$ ⑥ $(8, 1\frac{1}{2})$
② $(4\frac{1}{2}, 2)$ ⑦ $(2,0)$
③ $(2, 7\frac{1}{2})$ ⑧ $(0,6)$
④ $(6\frac{1}{2}, 3)$ ⑨ $(1\frac{1}{2}, 2\frac{1}{2})$
⑤ $(1,4)$ ⑩ $(8\frac{1}{2}, 4\frac{1}{2})$

Plotting Co-ordinates

D Draw a grid 10 across by 10 up, plot these points and join them
in the order they are given.

(9,2)   (6,3)   (8,2)
(8,0)   (4,4)   (6,3)
(3,0)   (4,7)   (6,2)
(2,1)   (6,6)   (9,2)
(1,3)   (6,7)   end
(4,3)   (6,6)
(4,2)   (8,5)
(6,2)

E Draw a grid 10 across by 6 up, plot the points and join them in the order they are given.

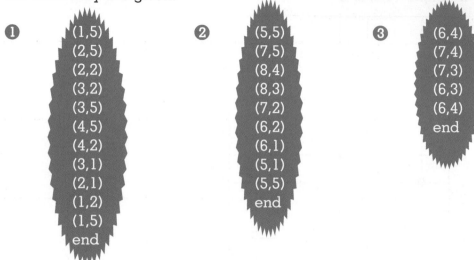

1
(1,5)
(2,5)
(2,2)
(3,2)
(3,5)
(4,5)
(4,2)
(3,1)
(2,1)
(1,2)
(1,5)
end

2
(5,5)
(7,5)
(8,4)
(8,3)
(7,2)
(6,2)
(6,1)
(5,1)
(5,5)
end

3
(6,4)
(7,4)
(7,3)
(6,3)
(6,4)
end

What word did you get?

F Draw a grid 15 across by 15 up, plot the co-ordinates of each shape and label them from the names given in the panel after you have joined up the co-ordinates.

Shape 1
(1,10)
(1,13)
(4,13)
(4,10)
(1,10)
-

Shape 3
(5,4)
(6,6)
(4,8)
(2,6)
(3,4)
(5,4)
-

Shape 5
(6,3)
(10,7)
(12,5)
(8,1)
(6,3)
-

Shape 2
(12,1)
(14,1)
(12,5)
(12,1)
-

Shape 4
(9,10)
(8,8)
(6,8)
(5,10)
(6,12)
(8,12)
(9,10)
-

rectangle

pentagon   hexagon

triangle   square

G Use the map to give the four-figure grid references of each named town.

Example Oakton ⇒ 19,42

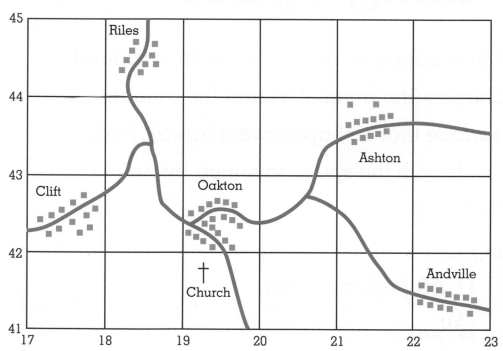

① Riles   ③ Ashton

② Clift   ④ Andville

Trace the map above and mark on each of the features.

Example Church ⇒ 19,41 (†)

⑤ tree at 20,44 (🌳)   ⑧ pond at 22,42 (🌑)

⑥ phone box at 18,43 (✆)   ⑨ hill top at 17,44 (▲)

⑦ marsh at 20,41 (🌿)

Checking your answers   Testing how much you know

Filling Space

This chapter is about the distance around shapes (the perimeter) and the amount of surface that a shape covers (area). It also deals with the space taken up by an object (volume).

Useful information

a **perimeter**

- the distance round the edge
- add up the lengths of all the sides
- measured in cm

b **area**

- the surface covered up by 2 D shapes
- the number of centimetre squares covered by a shape
- measured in centimetre squares (cm²)

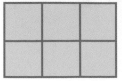

area → **6 centimetre squares = 6 cm²**

Ch 6 Shapes 1
Ch 7 Shapes 2
Ch 9 Units 1
Ch 22 Units 2
Ch 32 Formulas

Ch 32 Formulas

EXTENSION: E8, E9, E14, E15, E16
WORKSHEET: W18

c volume

– the space taken up by a 3-D shape
– the number of centimetre cubes taken up by a shape
– measured in centimetre cubes (cm³)

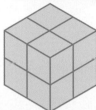

volume → 8 centimetre cubes = 8 cm³

Perimeters

A Draw these shapes on centimetre squared paper and find their perimeter.

Example

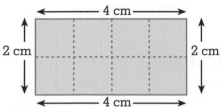

perimeter ⇒
4 + 2 + 4 + 2 = 12 cm

①

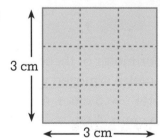

3 cm

3 cm

③

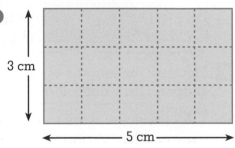

3 cm

5 cm

②

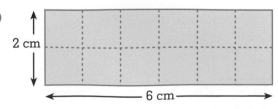

2 cm

6 cm

④

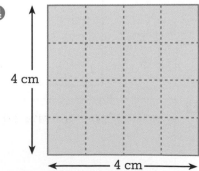

4 cm

4 cm

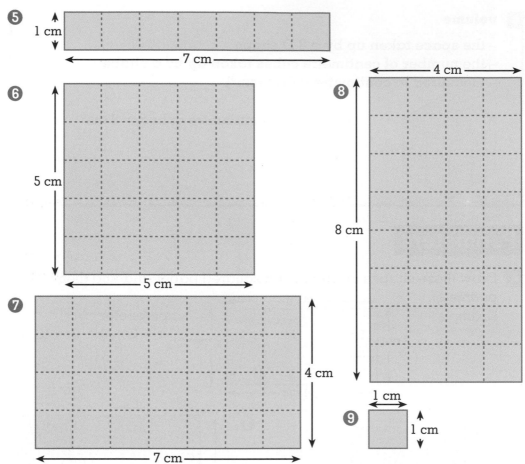

⑤ 1 cm ↕ ← 7 cm →

⑥ 5 cm ← 5 cm →

⑦ 4 cm ← 7 cm →

⑧ ← 4 cm → 8 cm

⑨ 1 cm ↔ 1 cm ↕

B Measure the lengths of each side to find the perimeter of these shapes. Draw each shape carefully onto centimetre squared paper.

Example

perimeter ⇒ 5 cm + 4 cm
+ 5 cm + 4 cm = 18 cm

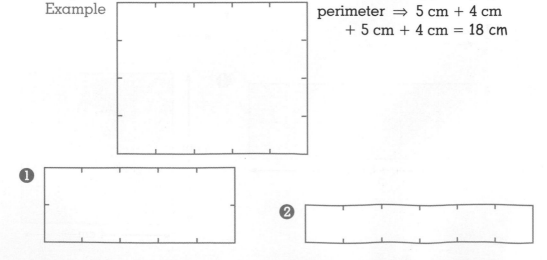

❶

❷

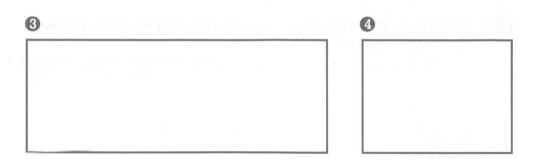

③ **④**

C Draw these shapes onto centimetre squared paper, label the length of each side and find the perimeter.

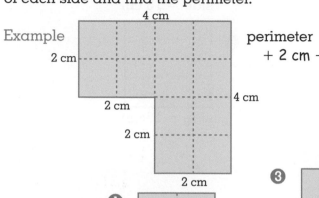

Example

4 cm

2 cm

2 cm

4 cm

2 cm

2 cm

perimeter ⟹ 4 cm + 4 cm + 2 cm
+ 2 cm + 2 cm + 2 cm = 16 cm

❶

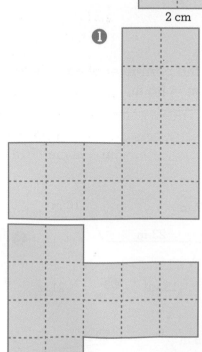

❷

❸

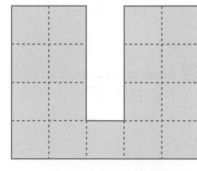

❹

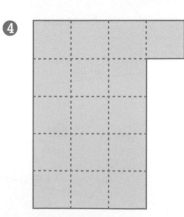

D Find the perimeter of each of these regular shapes. (Hint: regular shapes have sides all the same length.)

Example perimeter ⇒ 4 cm + 4 cm + 4 cm + 4 cm + 4 cm = 20 cm

side = 4 cm

1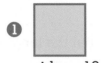

side = 12 cm

2

side = 7 m

3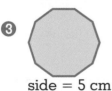

side = 5 cm

4

side = 13 cm

5

side = 15 cm

E Look at this map of a farm and find the perimeter of each field.

Example 27 m + 20 m + 19 m + 30 m = 96 m

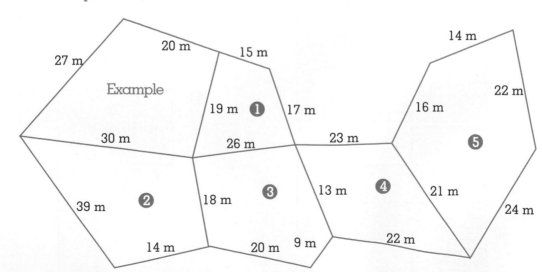

Areas

F Draw each shape and find the area by adding the centimetre squares.

Example

1	2	3
4	5	6

area ⇒ 6 cm squares (cm²)

❶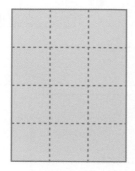

❷

❸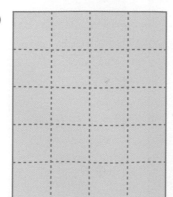

❹

❺

❻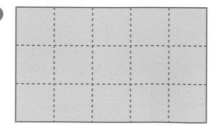

G Measure the length of each side and draw the shapes onto centimetre squared paper. Add the centimetre squares to find the area.

Example

area ⇒ 16 cm squares (cm²)

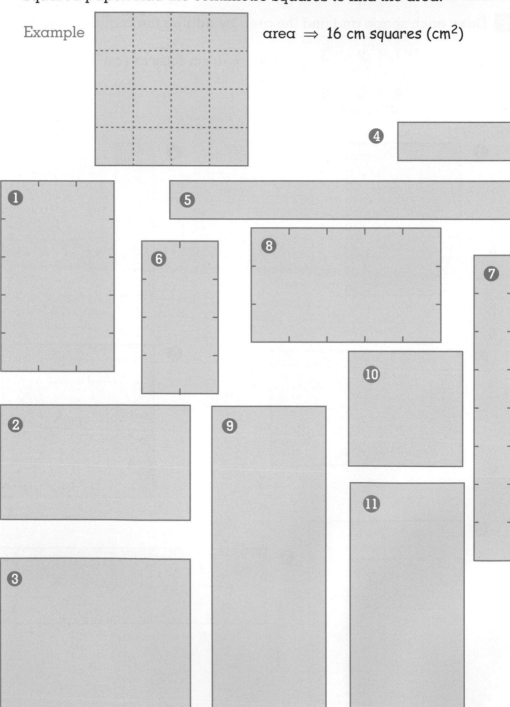

H Find the area of each of these shapes by counting centimetre squares (cm^2).

Example   area $\Rightarrow$ **7 cm squares (cm^2)**

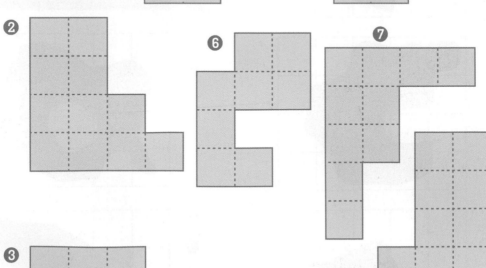

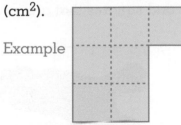

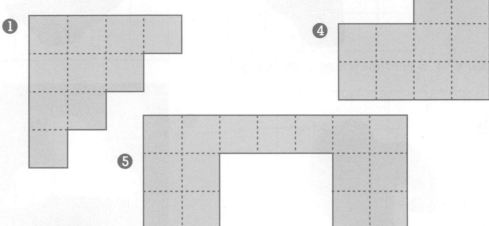

I Use worksheet (18) to estimate the shaded area of these shapes in centimetre squares. Count full squares and squares that are greater than a half as 1 cm².

Example

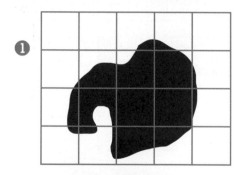

area ⇒ 8 centimetre squares (cm²)

❹

❶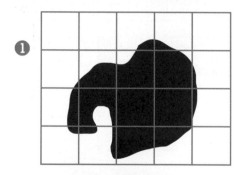

❺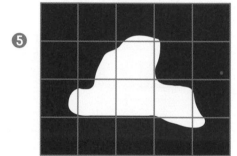

❷

❻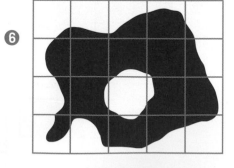

❸

❼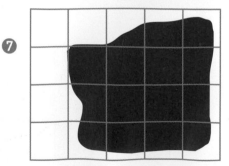

J Measure the length and width of each rectangle in cm and use the formula to work out the area in centimetre squares or cm^2.

area = length × width

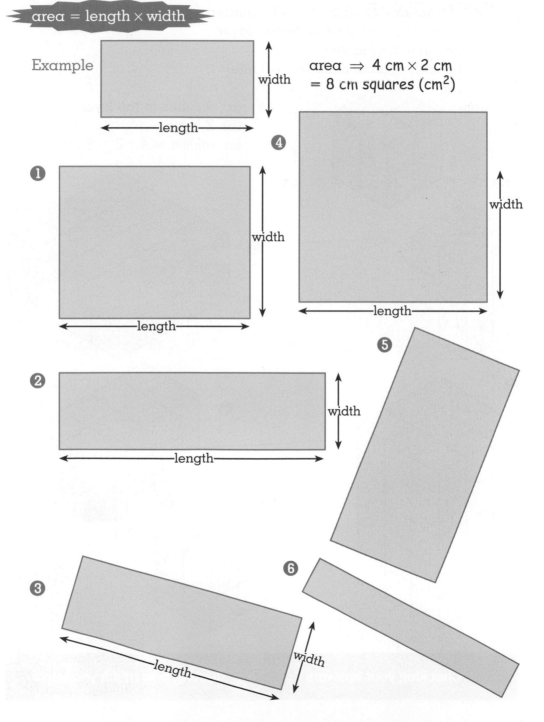

Example

area ⇒ 4 cm × 2 cm = 8 cm squares (cm^2)

width

length

1 width

length

2 width

length

4 width

length

5

6 width

3 length

width

Volume

K Find the volume of each shape by finding:
  (a) the number of cubes in the top layer
  (b) the number of layers
  (c) the total number of cubes (volume)

Example

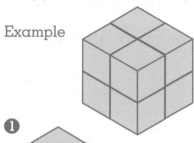

⇒ (a) 4 cubes in top layer
   (b) 2 layers
   (c) volume = 4 × 2 = 8 cubes

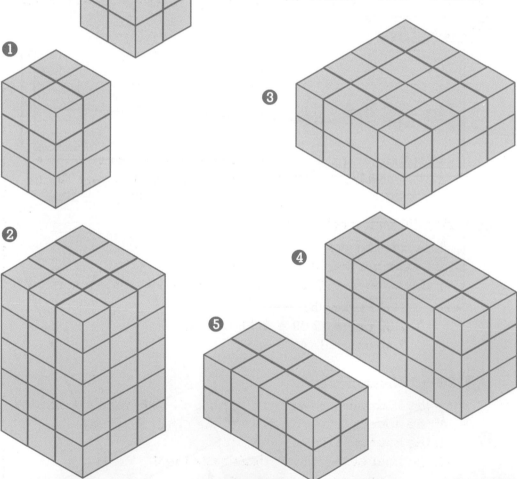

Time 2

This chapter is about changing from am and pm to 24 hour clock times, and the other way round. It also covers finding information from timetables.

10 Graphs and Tables 1
Ch 24 Time 1
25 Graphs and Tables 2

Useful information

a 24 hour clock times always have 4 digits. Hours and minutes can have a ':', '.' or nothing at all between them

b 12 → 24 hour clock
  – lose am and pm
  – if it was pm then add on 12 hours
  – if it was before 10 am then put a 0 in front of the hours
  e.g. 10.15 am → 10.15
       2.30 pm → 12.00 + 2.30 = 14.30
       7.45 am → 07.45

c 24 → 12 hour clock
  – if the hours are more than 12, take off 12 hours and add pm
  – if the hour is 12, leave hours alone but still add pm
  – if the hour is 11 or less, add am
  – if the hour starts with 0, don't write the 0
  e.g. 15.15 → 15.15 – 12.00 = 3.15 pm
       12.20 → 12.20 pm
       10.45 → 10.45 am
       06.30 → 6.30 am

24 Hour Clock

A Change these times to times on the 24 hour clock.
Example 10.00 am ⟹ 10.00

1 12.00 am
2 7.00 am
3 3.00 am
4 1.00 pm
5 3.00 pm

6 6.00 pm
7 8.00 pm
8 9.00 pm
9 11.00 pm

B Change these times back to the am and pm times.
Example 11.00 ⟹ 11.00 am

1 06.00
2 01.00
3 04.00
4 14.00
5 16.00

6 19.00
7 22.00
8 17.30
9 05.30

C Write down times from the bubble that are the same as each of these questions.
Example 21.15 ⟹ 9.15 pm

1 1.30 pm
2 07.45
3 2.55 am
4 3.40 pm
5 17.05
6 10.25 am
7 7.45 pm
8 09.15
9 11.50 pm
10 3.40 am

9.15 pm

19.45   10.25
15.40
23.50   5.05 pm
7.45 am   03.40
02.55
13.30
9.15 am

D Change the times that this train arrives at each station into 24 hour clock times.

	station	time of arrival am and pm time	24 hour clock
Example	Swansea	9.40 am	09.40
❶	Neath	9.53 am	
❷	Bridgend	10.14 am	
❸	Cardiff	10.42 am	
❹	Newport	11.05 am	
❺	Bristol	11.37 am	
❻	Swindon	12.18 am	
❼	Reading	1.07 pm	
❽	London	1.39 pm	

E Change the start time of these TV programmes from the 24 hour clock to am and pm times.

	station	start time am and pm time	24 hour clock
Example	breakfast show	7.15 am	07.15
❶	weather		08.55
❷	news		09.00
❸	chat to a star		09.40
❹	game time		10.25
❺	today's debate		11.10
❻	news		13.00
❼	cartoons		13.25
❽	film – *The Duke*		13.55
❾	tennis		15.40
❿	soap stars		17.05
⓫	children's drama		17.35

Timetables

F This table shows the times of sunrise and sunset in Exeter and Glasgow during a week in winter. Answer the questions below.

day	sunrise		sunset	
	Exeter	Glasgow	Exeter	Glasgow
Monday	08.02	08.13	17.13	16.59
Tuesday	08.00	08.12	17.14	17.01
Wednesday	07.59	08.10	17.16	17.02
Thursday	07.58	08.08	17.18	17.03
Friday	07.56	08.07	17.19	17.05
Saturday	07.54	08.05	17.20	17.07
Sunday	07.53	08.03	17.21	17.08

Example What time is sunset in Glasgow on Wednesday? ⇒ 17.02

❶ What time is sunrise in Exeter on Sunday?
❷ What time is sunrise in Glasgow on Friday?
❸ What time is sunset in Exeter on Tuesday?
❹ How long after sunrise in Exeter is sunrise in Glasgow on Tuesday?
❺ Copy and complete this table showing the differences in sunrise and sunset at Exeter and Glasgow.

day	sunrise differ ence	sunset differ ence
Monday	11 mins	
Tuesday		13 mins
Wednesday		
Thursday		
Friday		14 mins
Saturday		
Sunday	10 mins	

G This table shows the lesson times for three school days. Answer the
questions below.

Example What time does the Art lesson start on Tuesday? ⇒ 9.10 am

	Monday	Tuesday	Wednesday
9.00			
9.10	Form	Form	Form
	Maths	Art	English
9.50			
	Science	Art	French
10.40			
11.00			
	English	Geography	History
11.45			
	RE	Maths	PE
12.30			
1.20			
1.30	Form	Form	Form
	D&T	Music	Maths
2.10			
	D&T	English	Science
2.50			
3.30	Geography	French	Drama

Morning | *Afternoon* (vertical labels at left)

① What time does the Geography lesson start on Monday?
② What time does the French lesson start on Wednesday?
③ What time does the Science lesson end on Monday?
④ How long is the English lesson on Tuesday?
⑤ How long is the Drama lesson on Wednesday?
⑥ How long is the History lesson on Wednesday?
⑦ How long is the Maths lesson on Tuesday?
⑧ How long is the Art lesson on Tuesday?
⑨ How long is the D & T lesson on Monday?

H Look at these cut-outs from a TV guide showing the programmes for one evening. Answer the questions below.

Example How long is the news on Channel 1?
⇒ 6.00 pm → 6.28 pm ⇒ 28 min

Channel 1	
6.00 pm	News
6.28 pm	Weather
6.30 pm	Local News
7.10 pm	Live Sport
9.15 pm	Chatshow
9.55 pm	Film
11.40 pm	Comedy Hour
12.40 pm	Close

Channel 2	
6.00 pm	Soap
6.25 pm	Drama Part 1
8.40 pm	News
9.25 pm	Drama Part 2
11.00 pm	Sport Highlights
11.55 pm	Close

❶ How long is the news on Channel 2?
❷ At what times does the film start and end?
❸ How long is the live sport?
❹ How long is the drama part 1?
❺ How long is the drama part 2?
❻ How long is the drama althogether?
❼ Which programme lasts 2 minutes?
❽ List the programmes which last exactly 40 minutes?
❾ How many news programmes are there on both channels?
❿ How long does Channel 1 news, weather and local news last altogether?
⓫ How long is the film?
⓬ How much later is the news on Channel 2 than on 1?
⓭ How many episodes of the sports highlights can be videoed onto a 3-hour tape?

I This timetable shows the time taken for a journey by different forms of transport. Answer the questions below.

town/city	train	plane	car	coach	bus
Bristol	07.50	09.10	08.30	09.00	07.40
Swindon	08.32	-	09.35	10.20	08.55
Reading	09.17	-	10.37	11.30	10.25
London	09.45	10.05	11.10	12.02	11.37

❶ How long does each form of transport take to travel from Bristol to London?

(a) train
(b) plane
(c) car
(d) coach
(e) bus

❷ List the different forms of transport in order of time taken to complete the journey from Bristol to London, shortest first.

J Look at this train timetable. Answer the questions overleaf.
Example At how many stations does the 07.50 from Waterloo stop?
4 stations ⇒ Vauxhall, Clapham Junction, Wimbledon and Epsom

station	time	time	time	time	time
Waterloo	07.50	09.10	10.30	12.15	14.40
Vauxhall	07.57	-	-	12.22	14.46
Queens Rd	-	-	-	12.24	14.48
Clapham Junction	08.02	09.23	-	12.27	14.52
Earlsfield	-	09.30	-	12.35	14.59
Wimbledon	08.15	09.35	10.50	12.39	15.03
Raynes Park	-	09.39	10.54	-	15.07
Motspur Park	-	09.41	10.56	-	15.10
Worcester Park	-	09.46	11.02	-	15.16
Stoneleigh	-	-	11.06	-	15.21
Ewell West	-	09.52	11.10	-	15.25
Epsom	08.37	09.58	11.17	13.02	15.33

d **range** – the difference between the largest and the smallest numbers in a list

e.g.   1, 3, 6, 2, 4, 3, 9

smallest = 1

largest = 9

range = 9 – 1 = 8

Mean

A All the items in the panel are sold by number. Use the panels to answer the questions.

Would you be surprised to find the items below?

Example 10 chicken pieces in a pack? ⇒ No, as 10 is close to 9

Toilet roll
Average 240 sheets

Chicken pieces
Average 9 pieces

Polypockets
Average 100 per pack

Breakfast cereal
Average 20 servings

Nails
Average 100 per box

Kitchen roll
Average 90 sheets

Brass screws
Average 25 per pack

❶   243 sheets in a toilet roll?
❷   70 nails in a box?
❸   92 sheets in a kitchen roll?
❹   150 sheets in a toilet roll?
❺   19 servings in a box of breakfast cereals?
❻   40 brass screws in a pack?
❼   17 chicken pieces in a pack?
❽   180 polypockets in a pack?
❾   21 cleaning cloths in a pack?

Cleaning cloths
Average 20 cloths

B Work out the average number for the numbers in each bubble.

Example

2
3   7
4

Total ⇒ 2 + 3 + 4 + 7 = 16
Average ⇒ 16 ÷ 4 = 4

❼

£5
£25
£15

❶

9
13
11

❹

3
8   5
8

❽
16 kg
22 kg   21 kg
21 kg

❷
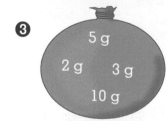
5 cm
2 cm   7 cm
6 cm

❺

10
9   2
14   5

❾
30 kg
50 kg
10 kg

❸
5 g
2 g   3 g
10 g

❻

17
21
22

❿
18 m
22 m   27 m
17 m

C Use a calculator to work out the average (mean) number in each of these questions.

Example 17, 14, 12, 11, 7, 19, 2, 6
Total ⇒ 17+14+12+11+7+19+2+6 = 88
Average ⇒ 88 ÷ 8 = 11

❶ 40, 30, 20, 70, 65, 45, 20, 90, 75, 45
❷ 100, 300, 700, 600, 800, 500
❸ 53, 72, 29, 48, 73, 67, 89, 49
❹ 4, 3, 5, 7, 9, 6, 8, 2, 10, 5, 5, 2, 7, 6, 11

D The table shows the takings for one week in 3 shops. Answer the questions below.

shop name	day of the week						
	Mon	Tues	Wed	Thurs	Fri	Sat	Sun
Newsbird	£70	£63	£48	£81	£73	£92	£66
Paperbird	£51	£77	£102	£93	£52	£70	£80
Sweetbird	£50	£37	£72	£51	£34	£51	£76

Work out the:
Example average takings in the 3 shops on Friday?
total $\Rightarrow$ £73 + £52 + £34 = £159
average $\Rightarrow$ £159 ÷ 3 = £53

1 average takings in the 3 shops on Wednesday
2 average daily takings in the Sweetbird shop
3 average takings in the 3 shops on Monday
4 average takings in the 3 shops on Thursday
5 average takings in the three shops on Sunday
6 average daily takings in the Paperbird shop
7 average takings in the 3 shops on Tuesday
8 average takings in the 3 shops on Saturday
9 average takings in the Newsbird shop
10 Which day had the best average takings?
11 Which shop had the worst average takings?

E Find the average temperature for the day from the graph

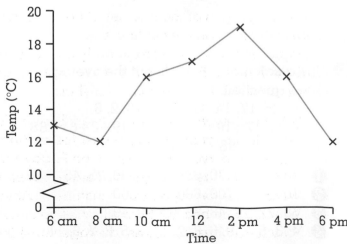

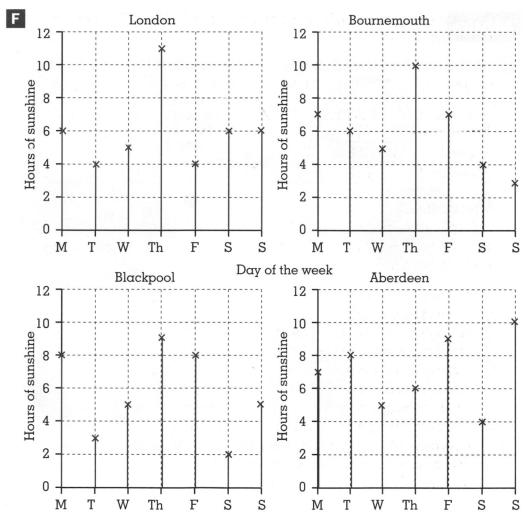

Use these graphs of the number of hours of sunshine in July to answer these questions in hours.

Example What is the average daily sunshine at Bournemouth?
total ⇒ 7 + 6 + 5 + 10 + 7 + 4 + 3 = 42
average ⇒ 42 ÷ 7 = 6 hours' sunshine

❶ What is the average sunshine on Sunday for the 4 places?
❷ What is the average daily sunshine at Blackpool?
❸ What is the average sunshine on Friday for the 4 places?
❹ Which day has the highest average sunshine?
❺ What is the average daily sunshine at Aberdeen?
❻ Which place has the highest average sunshine?
❼ Which day has the lowest average sunshine?

Mode

G Put the numbers in each barrel in order, smallest first, and find the mode.

Example

1, 1, 2, 2, 2, 3, 3, 3, 3, 4
There are two 1s
three 2s
four 3s
one 4
So 3 is the mode

Barrel example: 1 2 3 3 4 2 3 1 2 3

❶ 5 8 9 8 9 7 9 7 9 7 8 5

❸ 40 50 30 70 50 90 50 60 80 20 70 40 50

❷ 11 14 15 13 17 13 12 16 14 14 12 14 13 12

❹ 7 4 9 1 3 2 9 8 7 5 1 8 4 4 2 6 3

H This is the result of throwing a die 50 times. Draw and complete the frequency table to find the mode.

1, 5, 2, 2, 3, 6, 4, 4, 5, 2, 3, 5, 1, 6, 6, 6, 2, 3
5, 4, 3, 3, 1, 6, 5, 2, 3, 4, 1, 5, 1, 3, 6, 5, 2, 2, 4
6, 1, 2, 3, 3, 2, 1, 6, 4, 3, 3, 2, 4

1		
2			
3		
4	
5		
6	

Median

I Put the numbers in each shape in order, smallest first, and find the median number.

Example

1, 2, <u>2</u>, 4, 6 ⇒ median is 2

①

③

②

④

J Write each list in order, smallest first, and find the median for each list.

① 1, 4, 2, 6, 9, 3, 8, 2, 7, 4, 1, 6, 9, 7, 4, 4, 8, 2, 3

② 12, 11, 18, 23, 16, 19, 12, 18, 24, 18, 21, 20, 18, 25, 27

③ 100, 300, 700, 500, 800, 200, 300, 500, 900, 500, 700

K Change this frequency table into a list of ordered numbers to find the median.

1	IIII I
3	III
5	IIII
7	IIII I
9	II

Range

L Find the smallest and largest number from each panel.
What is the range of numbers in each panel?

Example

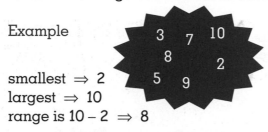

smallest ⇒ 2
largest ⇒ 10
range is 10 − 2 ⇒ 8

4

1

5

2

6

3

7

Average, Mode, Median and Range

M Use this table of marks in tests (all out of 10) to answer the questions below.

Name	English	Maths	Science	French	History	IT	RE
			Subjects				
Jim	7	7	9	4	6	8	8
Lucy	5	6	7	10	10	8	3
Anya	9	7	8	4	2	2	3

What is:

Example Jim's average mark $\Rightarrow$ 7 + 7 + 9 + 4 + 6 + 8 + 8
= 49 ÷ 7 = 7

❶ Lucy's median mark?
❷ Anya's modal mark?
❸ the average Science mark?
❹ the modal Maths mark?
❺ the median RE mark?
❻ the range of Lucy's marks?
❼ the range of History marks?
❽ the mean English mark?
❾ the mean History mark?

N Use the table in **M** to copy and complete the table below.

	average	mode	median	range
Jim	7			
Lucy			7	
Anya		2		